THE ESSENTIAL
PASTA
BOOK

100 perfect pasta recipes

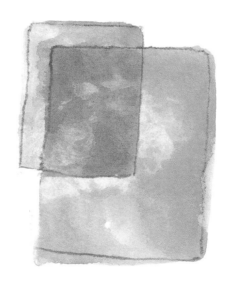

THE ESSENTIAL PASTA BOOK

100 perfect pasta recipes

Lesley Waters

with illustrations by Ken Cox

WEIDENFELD & NICOLSON
LONDON

Deepest thanks go to Louise
Wooldridge for her invaluable
help, support and friendship

First published in Great Britain in 1999
by Weidenfeld & Nicolson

Weidenfeld & Nicolson
Illustrated Division
Wellington House
125 Strand
London WC2R 0BB

Contents

Introduction
The Pasta Revolution

If I think back to my first taste of pasta, it was probably in tomato sauce, out of a tin and served on toast. A lot has happened in 30 years and although I'm still not averse to opening the odd tin, the choice of pasta (and I am including oriental noodles here, too) today is outstanding. We are spoilt for choice. Next time you go into a supermarket, take five minutes to look at what's available in the pasta department - virtually every week a new type appears. Fresh or dried, flavoured or plain, twisted or straight, big or small - whatever its origin, pasta has arrived and is here to stay.

So where did it all begin? There has been a lot written about who invented pasta. Some say it was the Italians, others say that Marco Polo introduced noodles from China to Italy. India and the Middle East also have early evidence of pasta, as do Ancient Greece, Spain and Russia. Whoever was the first, most cultures appear to have influenced pasta in one form or another. Undoubtedly the Italians are the leaders, however, when it comes to the production and cooking of pasta.

Pasta is a dough: a paste made up of flour, water and sometimes egg. An excellent carrier of flavour it can be boiled, baked or even deep-fried. There are lots of rules as to which pasta should be eaten with which sauce. Try not to get too bogged down in this - in my opinion you should cook your favourite pasta to your liking and eat it with your chosen sauce. THE ESSENTIAL PASTA BOOK contains over 100 recipes, from modern classics to the unexpected - dishes for all occasions and influenced by many cultures. But before you head for the kitchen, take time out to read the tips in the Perfect Pasta section (page 8), which will ensure successful pasta every time.

Without a doubt, pasta has revolutionized our meal times. We have embraced this simple paste with its chequered history. Long may it remain.

Lesley Waters

Perfect Pasta

Pasta is the ultimate convenience food. Easy and simple to cook and ready in minutes, it requires no special skills or fancy equipment. But as easy as it is to cook, it is to ruin - timing and technique are crucial. So before heading for the kitchen, take time out to read the following chapter. Packed with basic and practical advice, these hints and tips will result in perfect pasta every single time.

WATER - Always cook your pasta in plenty of boiling water. I use at least 1.2 litres (2 pints) for 115g (4oz) pasta. Make sure that the pasta is completely immersed in the water.

SALT - Adding salt to your pasta water will flavour it; some cooks swear by it but the choice is entirely yours. It is simply a matter of taste.

OIL - Some people choose to add oil to the pan when cooking to prevent the pasta from sticking. I have tried this on occasion but am not convinced that it makes much difference as the oil always seems to float to the top of the water, which seems a terrible waste of good olive oil. If you really like the idea of oil on your pasta, it is much better to add it after draining.

THE PLUNGE - To bring your water rapidly to a rolling boil, cover the pan with a lid. Remove the lid to add your pasta all at once. Cover with the lid again until the pasta returns to the boil. Remove the lid and stir the pasta once, then cook, uncovered, for the remaining cooking time, stirring your pasta from time to time during cooking, to help prevent it sticking.

LENGTHY PASTA - Some cooks believe that spaghetti or long strands of pasta should never be broken, but simply bent, while others think it makes no difference. If you don't want to snap your pasta, place it in a pan of boiling water and gently push on it. It will bend slightly and eventually be submerged. Be sure to give it a good stir to stop it sticking together.

AL DENTE - Traditionally, pasta is cooked until 'al dente', or 'to the tooth'. This means that it retains some of its bite. It should not, however, be undercooked and chalky. To test when your pasta is cooked, don't rely simply on the packet instructions. At the earliest time given, start testing. The only way to test your pasta is by lifting out a piece and tasting it. Keep testing the pasta every 30 seconds until it is 'al dente' or to your liking!

STUFFED PASTA - When cooking stuffed pasta such as ravioli or tortellini, keep the water at a very gentle boil. This will prevent any of the pasta from opening and the stuffing escaping into the water.

COOKING TIMES - Commercial fresh pasta is very quick to cook. Cooked in the same way as dried, in a large pan of boiling water, the timings will depend on the thickness and the shape of the pasta. Very thin pasta noodles may take as little as 30 seconds, tagliatelle or spaghetti about 1 minute and stuffed pastas such as ravioli or tortellini take about 5 minutes. Always check the packet instructions as these timings do differ from brand to brand. Start testing at the minimum time given on the packet (see 'Al dente' above).

Commercial dried pasta takes considerably longer to cook than fresh. Again, as a general rule, linguini and tagliatelle will take about 6-8 minutes and penne and rigatoni about 10-12 minutes. The thinner the pasta, the quicker it will cook. But, once again, check your packet for instructions and start testing for 'doneness' at the minimum time given.

STOP COOKING AND DRAIN QUICKLY - When your pasta is perfectly cooked to your liking, stop the process immediately by adding a cup of cold water to the pan. Drain your pasta quickly and briefly to prevent too much drying out and sticking. Some water should remain on your pasta and always reserve a little of the cooking water in case your pasta becomes overdrained and dry. This liquid can then be used to moisten and unstick your pasta if necessary.

MIXING IT - When mixing pasta with a sauce, toss it briefly and quickly. Too much air will rapidly cool down your pasta.

HOW MUCH PASTA PERSON? - As a guide, allow 55g (2oz) dried pasta per person for a starter or 85-115g (3-4oz) for a main course serving. When using fresh pasta, allow 55-85g (2-3oz) for a starter and 115-140g (4-5oz) for a main course. When serving fresh ravioli or

tortellini, you may wish to allow up to 140-175g (5-6oz) as a main course serving.

FRESH VERSUS DRIED - Don't write off dried pasta as being inferior to fresh. Good-quality dried pasta is often far better than the fresh variety. Look for Italian-made products made with durum wheat. They may cost a little extra but it will be well worth it. Fresh pasta can be made at home or is now readily

available in most supermarkets. It has a softer, more absorbent texture than dried and is at its best when stuffed, for example tortellini, ravioli or cannelloni.

NUTRITION - Pasta is a nutritious food. Even in its most basic form, when made from semolina and durum wheat, it is high in carbohydrate, low in fat and contains some protein. Its protein content can be increased with the addition of egg to the pasta dough.

CONVENIENCE - Satisfying and nourishing, pasta is the ultimate convenience food. In its dried form, it is a good-value item for your storecupboard, and quick and easy to cook for an instant hearty meal.

CHOOSING DRIED PASTA - When buying pasta, it is best to choose Italian brands since, by Italian law, pasta must be made with 100% durum (hard) wheat. This contains less starch, is higher in protein and is far superior to pasta made with soft, refined white flour. Dried pasta can be made with durum wheat and water only, or eggs can be added to the dough for richness and colour. Search out the best brands in your supermarket or local delicatessen.

LOW FAT - Pasta in itself is not that fattening. The calories come with the added accompaniments.

STORAGE - Store your dried pasta in a dry, dark cupboard and it will keep for over a year. Fresh pasta has a much shorter shelf life and should be kept refrigerated. Fresh pasta can be frozen quite successfully for approximately one month.

REHEATING - As a general rule, reheating pasta or noodles is not that successful, with the exception of lasagne and cannelloni dishes. Cooked pasta shells can be easily dressed to make a quick salad or try one of the recipes in this book for leftover pasta such as pasta pasties (see page 130).

LA FINE

useful equipment

There are a number of items you will find particularly useful for cooking pasta dishes and all are easily available.

• A good heavy-bottomed pan with tall sides and a lid. The pan should be big enough to hold 1.2 litres (2 pints) of water for every 115g (4oz) pasta. Stainless steel or the non-stick pans are the best ones to use.

• A large slotted spoon for lifting out pasta to test whether it is cooked.

• A long-handled wooden spoon to give your pasta a good stir and prevent it from sticking.

• A few knives are well worth investing in. A large chopping knife and a small vegetable knife, both of which should be kept sharp.

• One - or preferably two - chopping boards. Keep one board separate and use it only for preparing raw meats.

• A generous-sized colander with a long handle and lots of holes for fast draining. If it has little feet and can stand on its own, it is even better.

• A large ladle for spooning out your favourite sauce or broth.

• A heavy-based or non-stick frying pan or griddle - perfect for searing and fast cooking.

• A large wok, ideal for stir-fry pasta dishes, or it can be used as a big saucepan.

• A good peeler or grater for slivering or grating fresh Parmesan cheese.

• A good pepper mill for seasoning your pasta with the best freshly ground black pepper.

Pasta & Noodles Unravelled

There has always been much discussion about which pasta goes best with which sauce. As a general guideline, long, thin strands like spaghetti or linguini work well with oil-based sauces or light dressings. Thicker ribbons, such as pappardelle or tagliatelle, can take a richer or creamier sauce. As for short pasta shapes, for example rigatoni or fusilli, meat or other rich sauces work well as the pasta shape is designed to trap the sauce. However, all this being said, don't feel too restricted. At the end of the day it's all about cooking your favourite pasta or noodles and combining it with your chosen ingredients.

Flavoured pasta

Pasta is available in a wide variety of flavours - from simple spinach verde to beetroot and black squid ink! Spinach and egg pastas are well known to us and have been available for years but, more recently, many new flavoured pastas, both dried and fresh, have found their way on to our shelves. Some almost look like works of art - with prices to match! But some are very reasonable and the dried ones make excellent storecupboard standbys. Flavours currently available include garlic and chilli, tomato and basil, and funghi (mushroom), among many others.

Dried squid ink pasta is another example. Mysterious and black, the pasta is flavoured and coloured with the ink of a squid. This designer-style pasta is not as fishy as you might think and its stunning good looks are its forte. It is becoming more widely available and can be bought in noodle, shell or rotelle (cartwheels) form.

Tricolore, meaning 'three-colour', pasta is available in fresh and dried form, in an egg, spinach and tomato mix. From penne and tagliatelle to rotelle and shells, such pasta is very eye-catching and makes excellent salad-style party dishes.

Other types of pasta

Pasta can also be bought in a stage halfway between dried and fresh - in a vacuum-packed form. This is fresh pasta that has been specially sealed to give it a longer shelf life. At first only available as stuffed tortellini, I have recently seen vacuum-packed pasta shells and spirals.

Brown, wholewheat pasta was originally available only as spaghetti, but can now be bought as pasta shapes. It has a slightly nutty taste and is best when tossed in simple butter- or oil-based sauces. An unrefined pasta, it takes longer to cook than the more usual pasta, so do read the packet instructions carefully. Corn pasta is a wheat- and gluten-free pasta, making it a good alternative for those allergic to wheat. The cooking method and times are as for wheat pasta and, as ever, beware not to overcook it.

Organic pasta is made in the

same way as normal pasta, but using organic durum wheat. As yet, only a limited range is available in Britain, but this is sure to change with the increasing popularity of organic foods.

Oriental noodles

Oriental noodles are a form of pasta, made from flour and water or from flour, water and eggs. The flour used can be made from be wheat, buckwheat, rice, soya or mung bean, and differs from the durum wheat used for authentic dried pasta. Noodles generally have a softer texture and come in many forms. These are lighter than pasta and can be cooked in minutes - steamed, stir-fried or cooked in broths. Sold dried in pressed packages or long bundles, some delicious oriental noodles are now sold fresh. Served in roughly the same quantities as given for pasta, noodles are excellent added to soups to make a satisfying meal.

Top 25 Pastas & Noodles

This directory includes the better-known types of pasta and noodles but there are many more - every week sees the arrival of yet another pasta or noodle, from brand new, easy-to-cook designs to more authentic, quality pastas. Take a trip to your delicatessen and explore the exciting possibilities.

ANGEL HAIR - Angel hair or capellini d'angelo pasta is very delicate, even more so than vermicelli. Buy it dried or fresh and use in soups or broths, or in baked dishes or served with a light sauce.

CANNELLONI - This can be bought as dried tubes, or you can make your own by stuffing and rolling fresh lasagne. Alternatively, buy fresh cannelloni, ready-rolled and stuffed, and simply serve it with your favourite sauce.

CAPPELLETTI - This is a fresh stuffed pasta, similar to tortellini but smaller. Serve it with a tomato sauce or dressed simply with Parmesan cheese, olive oil and freshly ground black pepper.

CASARECCIE - These short strips of dried pasta with a twist have recently appeared in our supermarkets. They are easy to eat and simple to toss with a tomato sauce.

CONCHIGLIE - This is a popular pasta, shaped like sea shells. Widely available, in various sizes and in both dried and fresh form, it is a perfect pasta for everyday use and is especially good with tomato-style ragout sauces. The largest pasta shells are ideal for stuffing. The smallest, called conchigliette or conchellini, are great in soups or can be used in stuffing. They also make an excellent first pasta for children.

EGG NOODLES - Available fresh or dried, and in a variety of widths - thin, medium and thick, these wheat-based Chinese noodles can be stir-fried, simmered in soups or tossed in a salad with sesame oil. Versatile and fast to cook, if dried, simply soak or simmer them in boiling water. Fresh egg noodles cook in seconds.

FARFALLE - These pasta butterflies or bow ties with fluted edges are a popular everyday dried pasta. Take care as this pasta doesn't always cook evenly - when the outer edge is cooked, the centre can sometimes still be hard. Farfalle is available in different sizes - look for farfallini (baby) or farfalloni (extra large).

FETTUCCINE - Slightly thinner than -and often mistaken for - tagliatelle, fettuccine is very good with rich creamy sauces and best when used fresh rather than dried.

FUSILLI - These attractive corkscrew twists are ideal sauce trappers as the sauce wraps around the pasta and clings to its spiral shape. Available both fresh and dried, the fresh makes an interesting crouton when deep-fried (see crispy pasta salad, page 111). This is another pasta that is available in baby form, called fusillini.

LASAGNE - These wide sheets of pasta are served either layered and baked, or open style. Dried lasagne can be bought with smooth or ruffled edges in plain, egg or spinach form. It requires boiling before use unless you purchase the precooked variety, which can be used straight from the packet. In this case, simply layer the dried pasta sheets with your chosen sauce, but be aware that this type of lasagne needs to be generously covered with sauce, to avoid a dry and disappointing

result. Fresh lasagne is more delicate and gives better results than the dried variety. It is now easily available.

LINGUNI - A type of flat spaghetti, the word 'linguini' means tongues. This pasta is the perfect partner to seafood sauces or dress it simply with a chillied oil and masses of black pepper. It is now available fresh and cooks in 1-2 minutes.

MACARONI - Don't just bake macaroni with cheese in the traditional way - it is a versatile, readily available dried pasta that works well with meat-based sauces, too. Quick-cook and baby versions can also be found and their hollow shells are excellent flavour trappers.

PAPPARDELLE - Made with eggs and semolina, these fabulous flat wide ribbons of pasta, which sometimes have a crimped edge, have a definite luxurious touch. Originally available as a plain dried pasta, it can now be bought fresh, plain or with added flavouring. Amazing with rich, creamy sauces and traditionally served with gamey-style sauces, pappardelle is just as good with a simple warm dressing.

PENNE - These short, diagonally cut ridged tubes are available both fresh and dried, and are excellent combined with hearty robust sauces or in pasta bakes.

RAVIOLI - Traditionally a way of using up leftovers or stuffed

with spinach and ricotta cheese, ravioli can now be bought with a variety of fillings. From pumpkin and pine nuts to smoked salmon and cream cheese, the range is vast and growing. Ravioli is great simmered in a broth or tossed in a tomato or cheesy sauce. Raviolini is a baby version of this pasta.

RICCIOLI - This is a form of open spiral pasta that can be bought fresh or dried and is great for entrapping a thick sauce. Deep-fried fresh riccioli makes an unusual pudding (see cinnamon & honey pasta with vanilla ice cream, page 136).

RICE NOODLES - These noodles are wheat-free and therefore good for anyone allergic to wheat.

They are normally found in thin angel hair form or as flat noodles. Thin rice noodles lend themselves best to dropping into clear soups. If you are lucky enough to find the flat noodles (fresh or dried), stir-fry them with fish and eggs (see pad Thai noodles, page 46).

RIGATONI - This dried pasta is one of my favourites: robust, ridged flat tubes that are great tossed with hearty sauces, especially bolognaise. The hollow insides are great for catching thick sauces and for using in oven-baked dishes.

RISI - These small rice-shaped grains are even smaller than conchigliette, and are great used in soups and broth.

SOBA NOODLES - These are a Japanese style of noodle, available dried - and in some supermarkets fresh and ready to stir-fry. Made from a mixture of buckwheat and wheat flour they are good in hot soups, coconut broth or stir-fried.

SPAGHETTI - Probably the first pasta to be seen in Britain, these pasta 'strings' are best when not oversauced or overdressed. Spaghetti is probably most often associated with bolognaise sauce, but purists would advocate a more traditional seafood sauce such as vongole. Equally delicious with tomato- or oil-based sauces, fresh spaghetti cooks in about 3 minutes.

TAGLIATELLE - These flat narrow noodles are available fresh or dried and in egg or spinach (verde) form. Both types can be found mixed together. A popular pasta, it is very good tossed in simple cream or butter sauces. Look out for tagliarini, which is a thinner version.

TORTELLINI - Similar to ravioli, but with a thicker, rounder, almost ear-like shape, tortellini is available fresh and dried. A carrier of many fillings, tortellini is cooked and served in a similar way to ravioli. For a modern touch, serve them as a canapé with a dipping sauce (see bloody Mary pasta, page 129).

VERMICELLI - Bought as nests of skinny pasta, vermicelli is fast cooking and versatile. Use it in its nest form, stirred into thick or clear soups; it is even light enough to use in a soufflé (see souffléed Stilton vermicelli with celery & apple relish, page 132). Look out for the excellent fresh variety, which cooks in just 1 minute.

YOKISOBA & UDON NOODLES These are two versions of Japanese-style noodles now available in vacuum-packed form, which are excellent in quick stir-fry dishes.

Secret ingredients

Here is a special selection of store-cupboard ingredients, which are particularly useful for instantly transforming plain pasta or noodles. Build up your store cupboard gradually by investing in a few of these jewels and soon you will have a treasure chest to delve into to create stunning dishes full of flavour.

BOTTLED ANTIPASTO - In recent years, these jars of prepared, cooked and marinated artichokes, mushrooms, peppers, aubergines, baby onions and seafood have become widespread. Drain the contents of a jar and toss through freshly cooked warm pasta, reserving the oil, if you wish, for cooking or for adding a little extra flavour.

OLIVES - There are many different types of olives. My favourites are the Greek-style black ones. These have a wrinkled skin and a softer texture than some olives, which are more bullet-like. Don't expect them to pit easily - they may come out looking a bit rough and ragged but it really doesn't matter.

ESSENTIAL OILS - Virgin olive oil is oil from the first pressing of the olives. Its flavour and structure can be altered by overheating or incorrect storage. Store all oil in containers with tight-fitting lids, out of direct sunlight and in a cool place. Olive oil is best used in light dressings or in dishes where the flavour will not be overpowered or overheated.

Walnut oil does not keep well, so buy it in small quantities and store in the same way as olive oil. It is delicious drizzled over roasted vegetables with pasta, or tossed through pasta, toasted walnut halves and crumbled Roquefort cheese.

Groundnut oil is a good all-round oil for dressings, stir-fries and spicy dishes. Surprisingly, it does not taste strongly of nuts and is excellent for using with other flavours.

Sun-dried tomato oil is great stirred sparingly through pasta with Parmesan cheese. Don't buy it specially if you already have a jar of sun-dried tomatoes in oil in your cupboard since you can use this oil.

Sesame oil is very rich and strong. Use it sparingly as an added seasoning rather than as a cooking oil.

PESTO SAUCES - These are good as a standby if you really don't have time to make your own (see the easy pesto recipes in the Speedy Suppers chapter). A massive range is now available - from sun-dried tomato to pepper and the classic basil pesto. Look out for the new creamy version of pesto, which has a lighter taste. Stir bottled pesto quickly through hot pasta and, once opened, keep refrigerated.

HARISSA - Use this spicy, Moroccan-style vegetable paste sparingly to pep up and add spice to home-made tomato dishes. Sold in jars or tubes, you will need to store it in the fridge after opening.

SUN-DRIED VEGETABLES - Sun-drying vegetables greatly intensifies their flavour, so a little goes a long way. The process started with tomatoes and has rapidly expanded so that the range now includes peppers, aubergines and chillies. Simply soak them in boiling water to rehydrate, according to the packet directions. Chop or slice the rehydrated vegetables, fry in a little flavoured oil and toss through freshly cooked pasta with fresh basil and grated Parmesan cheese.

DRIED WILD MUSHROOMS - They might seem expensive but, like sun-dried vegetables, a little goes a long way. Soak dried mushrooms for at least 20-30 minutes in boiling water and strain through kitchen paper. Use them in sauces or chop, fry in butter and toss through pasta.

CANNED CHERRY TOMATOES
The ever-popular canned tomato makes an excellent quick sauce base. If you cannot get cherry tomatoes, buy chopped tomatoes in rich tomato juice as a tasty alternative.

SUN-DRIED TOMATO PASTE - Puréed sun-dried tomatoes with oil is the modern and far superior version of traditional tomato purée. It is excellent for an intense and slightly sweet tomato flavour. Once opened, keep it refrigerated.

TRUFFLE PASTE - This is another concentrated flavour, generally made from the Italian white truffle. It is superb when heated sparingly with cream and tossed through pasta.

RED AND GREEN THAI CURRY PASTES - These pastes are an excellent alternative to spending hours with your pestle and mortar, grinding together the classic Thai flavours of lemon grass, chillies, galangal, shrimp paste, shallots and garlic. There are many different brands and all differ in intensity: some can be very hot, so taste a little before you use. Thai curry paste is wonderful fried briefly in a little oil and mixed with coconut milk as a broth base for noodles (see green coconut broth with chicken & soba noodles, page 44).

JUNIPER BERRIES - These berries give a strong pungent flavour reminiscent of gin. Crush them lightly, using the back of a wooden spoon, and use in a hot dressing or in a warm creamy sauce to accompany smoked fish and pasta.

COCONUT MILK AND CREAM
Coconut milk or cream is not the milk from the centre of the coconut, but a liquid made from the flesh. Coconut cream (available in cartons) is both richer and thicker than coconut milk (available in cans) and comes from the first pressing of the coconut flesh. If neither is available, buy creamed coconut in a block, grate or chop it and mix with water.

BALSAMIC VINEGAR - Balsamic vinegar is made from grape juice and is aged in wooden casks in Italy. It has a slightly sweet flavour with a gentle sour kick and a few drops is enough to appreciate its intensity. Don't just use it as a dressing ingredient - it works in sauces, soups or stews with pasta.

RICE VINEGAR - Rice vinegar is made from distilled rice wine. Of Chinese and Japanese origin, it can differ greatly from country to country. Some rice vinegars are quite sharp, while others are gentle and sweeter.

CAPERS - These buds from a Mediterranean bush can be bought as large or baby berries and are preserved in vinegar or just salt. They are wonderful in tapenades or fried in butter with chopped anchovies and tossed with hot pasta.

KAFFIR LIME LEAVES - These are a classic Thai ingredient, which are now available fresh or dried. If you find a supply of fresh kaffir lime leaves, buy them and freeze until required. Use them as you would a bay leaf to give a citrus kick - sliced if fresh or crumbled if dried.

GENTLEMAN'S RELISH - This spiced anchovy relish makes an excellent condiment. Heat a little in cream, add a handful of parsley and toss it through hot pasta. Season if you like with black pepper but do not use salt since, like canned anchovies, it is very salty.

DRIED SEAWEED - This vegetable from the Japanese seas is highly nutritious. There are many different types and most require presoaking for 10-20 minutes, unless you are adding them to soups or stews. Dried seaweed is a delicious addition to noodle soups or to stir-fries.

FISH SAUCE (NAM PLA) - A basic flavouring in Thai cooking, this is now available in supermarkets in bottled form. It is made from fermented fish or seafood and gives a distinctive, slightly salty flavour.

SOY SAUCE - Available light or dark, soy sauce can be used as an accompaniment or as an ingredient. Dark soy sauce is slightly thicker and sweeter, while the light soy sauce is a

little saltier. The latter can be used in place of fish sauce if necessary.

BLACK BEAN SAUCE - Made from fermented black beans, this rich sauce can be bought in jars or, even better, fresh. The latter may not be as strong as the bottled version but is infinitely prefereable. It is excellent with fish in oriental dishes.

SICHUAN/SZECHUAN PEPPERCORNS - These Chinese peppercorns, reddish brown in colour, are best used dry-roasted in a frying pan and then crushed to release their full pungent flavour, before adding them to your dish. They are excellent served with beef and pasta (see Sichuan beef noodles, page 48).

CANNED CRAB, MUSSELS, OYSTERS AND CLAMS - Canned crab and clams are a wonderful, quick way of adding an instant taste of seafood to your pasta or noodle dishes. Smoked mussels and oysters in oil are now available, and have a far superior taste to those in sold in brine.

LUMPFISH ROE - These lumpfish eggs may not sound that attractive, but come in black or orange and look stunning. This 'poor man's caviare' should not be ignored - use it at the last minute to add a final flourish to your dish.

PARMESAN CHEESE - Gone are the days of the smelly dried powder that only vaguely resembled this king of Italian cheeses. This classic accompaniment for pasta can be bought ready grated, but I would always recommend freshly grating or shaving it yourself. Invest in the best Parmesan Reggiano and store it loosely wrapped in greaseproof paper and foil in the fridge. If it is young, use a good peeler for shavings, while the more mature and drier cheeses are better for grating. You will find your pasta needs nothing more.

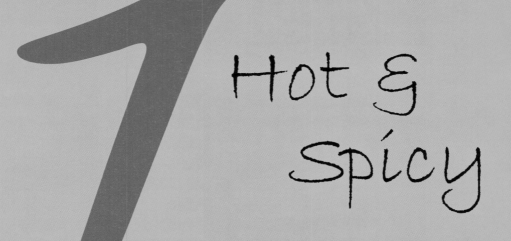

Hot & Spicy

Curried, spiced and chillied, the heat is on! Thai, Indian, Chinese and Spanish dishes, normally served with rice, are partnered with pasta in this collection and prove you shouldn't just serve pasta the traditional Italian way. It goes wonderfully with chillies and spices, too, so don't miss out - spice it up!

Whether you like things really hot or just with a hint of extra spice, these recipes will bring zest to your cooking and dining. Sichuan peppercorns, red chillies, Thai curry paste, cardamom, coriander, cumin and even chocolate are some of the flavours that enhance these pasta dishes, making them something out of the ordinary. So start by extending the boundaries of what you expect from pasta and bring some heat into the kitchen.

Pasta picada

SERVES 4

600ML (1 PINT) WATER

150ML (¼ PINT) WHITE WINE

1 BAY LEAF

1 TEASPOON CUMIN SEEDS

225G (8OZ) CARROTS, SLICED

225G (8OZ) SUGAR SNAP PEAS

115G (4OZ) PETIT POIS

1 X 400G (14OZ) CAN CHICKPEAS, DRAINED

350G (12OZ) DRIED LARGE PASTA SHELLS

2 TABLESPOONS CHOPPED FRESH FLAT-LEAF
    PARSLEY, TO GARNISH

SALT AND FRESHLY GROUND BLACK PEPPER

FOR THE PICADA

25G (1OZ) HAZELNUTS, ROASTED

25G (1OZ) PINE NUTS, TOASTED

1 LARGE THICK SLICE BREAD, CUBED AND FRIED
    IN OLIVE OIL

1 CLOVE GARLIC

2 TABLESPOONS CHOPPED FRESH FLAT-LEAF
    PARSLEY

1. Place the water, wine, bay leaf and cumin seeds in a large pan and bring to the boil. Season with salt and stir in the carrots. Simmer for 7-8 minutes.

2. Add the sugar snap peas, petit pois and chickpeas. Simmer for 6 more minutes, or until the vegetables are just tender.

3. Meanwhile, make the picada. Grind the nuts in a food processor or liquidizer. Add the fried bread cubes, garlic and flat-leaf parsley and blend to form a paste. Thin the paste by adding 1-2 tablespoons of the vegetable cooking liquid.

4. Cook the pasta shells in a pan of boiling water as directed on the packet.

5. Stir the picada into the vegetable stew and simmer for 4-5 minutes, adding a little water if necessary, and season to taste.

6. To serve, drain the pasta well and transfer to serving bowls. Spoon over the picada stew and scatter with chopped parsley.

PICADA IS A SAVOURY PASTE USED IN SPAIN TO ADD THICKNESS AND FLAVOUR. THIS VEGETABLE PICADA STEW MAKES AN UNUSUAL ACCOMPANIMENT FOR LARGE PASTA SHELLS.

Cauliflower & chilli

SERVES 4

1 TABLESPOON OLIVE OIL

4 RASHERS BACON, CHOPPED

150ML (¼ PINT) WHITE WINE

150ML (¼ PINT) VEGETABLE STOCK

1 RED CHILLI, FINELY CHOPPED

450G (1LB) LARGE CAULIFLOWER FLORETS

350G (12OZ) DRIED LARGE SPINACH PASTA
   SHELLS

55G (2OZ) GRUYÈRE CHEESE, GRATED

1 BUNCH FRESH FLAT-LEAF PARSLEY, CHOPPED

SALT AND FRESHLY GROUND BLACK PEPPER

1. Heat the oil in a large pan. Add the chopped bacon and fry for 5 minutes.

2. Stir in the wine, stock and finely chopped chilli and cook for 5 minutes. Add the cauliflower and season well. Cover and steam for 8-10 minutes, until the cauliflower is cooked.

3. Meanwhile, cook the pasta in a pan of boiling water as directed on the packet.

4. To serve, drain the pasta and toss with the chillied cauliflower, Gruyère and flat-leaf parsley. Transfer to serving bowls, scatter with a little more parsley and serve at once.

CAULIFLOWER, GRUYÈRE CHEESE AND BIG PASTA SHELLS ARE TRANSFORMED BY THE ADDITION OF RED CHILLI IN THIS WARMING DISH!

Baked garlic mushrooms with red hot tomato sauce

SERVES 4

4 LARGE FIELD MUSHROOMS, STALKS REMOVED

3 TABLESPOONS OLIVE OIL

1 CLOVE GARLIC, CRUSHED

SQUEEZE OF LEMON JUICE

280G (10OZ) FRESH LINGUINI

1 QUANTITY RED HOT TOMATO SAUCE
  (SEE PAGE 80)

1 TABLESPOON CHOPPED FRESH FLAT-LEAF
  PARSLEY

SALT AND FRESHLY GROUND BLACK PEPPER

FOR THE STUFFING

25G (1OZ) BUTTER

3 RASHERS SMOKED BACK BACON, DICED

1 CLOVE GARLIC, CRUSHED

55G (2OZ) FRESH WHITE BREADCRUMBS

2 TABLESPOONS CHOPPED FRESH PARSLEY

1. Toss the mushrooms in the oil, garlic and lemon juice. Season with black pepper and set aside, gills uppermost, in a shallow ovenproof dish, for 30 minutes.

2. Preheat the oven to Gas Mark 6/200°C/400°F.

3. To make the stuffing, heat the butter in a frying pan. Add the bacon and garlic and fry for 5 minutes. Add the breadcrumbs and chopped parsley and season.

4. Spoon the bacon and garlic stuffing on to the marinated mushrooms. Bake in the oven for 25-30 minutes until golden and cooked, covering with a sheet of foil if the stuffing becomes too browned.

5. Meanwhile, cook the pasta in a pan of boiling water as directed on the packet and gently heat the red hot tomato sauce.

6. To serve, drain the pasta and toss briefly with the red hot tomato sauce. Spoon into 4 serving dishes and top each with a baked garlic mushroom. Scatter over a little chopped parsley and serve at once.

MUSHROOMS MARINATED IN AND STUFFED WITH GARLIC! SERVE ON TOMATO-DRESSED LINGUINI AND SERVE AS A LIGHT LUNCH.

Spanish chillied pasta

SERVES 4

2 TABLESPOONS OLIVE OIL

1 LARGE ONION, CHOPPED

1 RED PEPPER, SLICED

450G (1LB) GOOD-QUALITY MINCED BEEF

1 CLOVE GARLIC, CRUSHED

2 HOT RED CHILLIES, DESEEDED AND FINELY
  CHOPPED, OR 2 TEASPOONS CHILLI SAUCE

1 x 420G (15OZ) CAN CHOPPED TOMATOES IN
  TOMATO JUICE

1 TABLESPOON TOMATO PURÉE

1 x 400G (14OZ) CAN KIDNEY BEANS, DRAINED
  AND RINSED

25G (1OZ) GOOD-QUALITY CONTINENTAL
  CHOCOLATE, GRATED

350G (12OZ) DRIED TAGLIATELLE

1 BUNCH FRESH FLAT-LEAF PARSLEY, CHOPPED

SALT AND FRESHLY GROUND BLACK PEPPER

1. Heat the oil in a large pan. Add the onion and red pepper and fry for 5 minutes until softened. Push the onion and pepper to the side of the pan, increase the heat and add the minced beef. Fry over a high heat for 2-3 minutes until browned.

2. Stir the mince, onions and pepper together, add the garlic and chillies and fry for 1 minute. Season well.

3. Add the chopped tomatoes, tomato purée and kidney beans. Bring to the boil, cover and simmer for 40 minutes. Then stir in the chocolate and simmer for a further 5 minutes.

4. To serve, cook the pasta in a pan of boiling water as directed on the packet. Drain and toss with the chopped parsley. Divide between 4 serving plates and top each with some of the hot chilli sauce. Serve at once.

IN SPAIN, CHOCOLATE IS ADDED TO RABBIT STEW; IN MEXICO THEY ADD IT TO CHILLI! THE RESULT IS A DELICIOUS RICHNESS AND NOT AS SWEET AS YOU MIGHT THINK.

Aromatic chicken with almonds & noodles

SERVES 4

1 TABLESPOON SUNFLOWER OR GRAPESEED OIL

2 LARGE ONIONS, CHOPPED

2 CLOVES GARLIC, CRUSHED

3 TEASPOONS TURMERIC

1 TABLESPOON MEDIUM MADRAS CURRY PASTE

3 LARGE CHICKEN BREASTS, CUT INTO 2.5CM
   (1 INCH) CUBES

200ML (7FL OZ) CHICKEN STOCK

JUICE OF ½ LEMON

1 KAFFIR LIME LEAF OR BAY LEAF

150ML (¼ PINT) DOUBLE CREAM

2 TABLESPOONS GROUND ALMONDS

250G (9OZ) MEDIUM EGG NOODLES

1 BUNCH FRESH CORIANDER, CHOPPED

55G (2OZ) TOASTED FLAKED ALMONDS

SALT AND FRESHLY GROUND BLACK PEPPER

1. Heat the oil in a large pan. Add the onions and fry for 4-5 minutes until softened.

2. Add the garlic, turmeric, curry paste and chicken pieces and cook for a further 4-5 minutes.

3. Stir in the stock, lemon juice and kaffir lime or bay leaf and season. Bring to the boil and simmer for 10-12 minutes, or until the chicken is just cooked.

4. Stir in the double cream and ground almonds and simmer for a further 5 minutes.

5. Meanwhile, cook the noodles in a pan of boiling water as directed on the packet.

6. To serve, drain the noodles and toss with the chopped coriander and flaked almonds. Divide between 4 serving plates. Spoon over the aromatic chicken and serve at once.

CHICKEN IS COOKED WITH GROUND ALMONDS, AND SERVED WITH EGG NOODLES TOSSED WITH CORIANDER AND FLAKED ALMONDS IN THIS NUTTY DISH.

Sweet & sour pork balls

SERVES 4

250g (9oz) MEDIUM EGG NOODLES

115g (4oz) BABY PAK CHOI

1 TABLESPOON SESAME OIL

FOR THE MEATBALLS

375g (12oz) MINCED PORK

85g (3oz) BREADCRUMBS

1 BUNCH OF SPRING ONIONS, FINELY CHOPPED

1 TABLESPOON TOMATO PURÉE

1 EGG

SALT AND FRESHLY GROUND BLACK PEPPER

FOR THE SWEET AND SOUR SAUCE

½ TABLESPOON GROUNDNUT OIL

1 LARGE CLOVE GARLIC, CRUSHED

2.5CM (1 INCH) ROOT GINGER, PEELED AND FINELY CHOPPED

4 TABLESPOONS WHITE WINE VINEGAR

2 TABLESPOONS TOMATO PURÉE

1 TABLESPOON SOY SAUCE

2 TABLESPOONS RUNNY HONEY

1 TABLESPOON CORNFLOUR, MIXED WITH 1 TABLESPOON WATER

4 TABLESPOONS COLD WATER

1. Preheat the oven to gas mark 6/200°C/400°F. Lightly grease a baking tray and set to one side.

2. Cook the egg noodles in a pan of boiling water as directed on the packet.

3. Place all the meatball ingredients in a food processor. Season well and whizz together. Form the mixture into 12 meatballs and place on the baking tray. Roast in the oven for 25-30 minutes until browned and cooked through.

4. Heat the groundnut oil in a pan. Add the garlic and ginger and gently fry for one minute. Add all the remaining sauce ingredients to the pan and stir together. Simmer for 2 minutes.

5. To serve, heat a wok or large pan. Wash the pak choi and add the wet leaves to the pan. Toss over the heat for 1-2 minutes until wilted. Add the cooked noodles and sesame oil and toss for a further 1-2 minutes until piping hot. Divide the hot noodles between four serving plates. Top with the meatballs and spoon over the hot sauce.

Prawn & chickpea pasta

SERVES 2

1 TABLESPOON GRAPESEED OR SUNFLOWER OIL

1 ONION, CHOPPED

1-2 TABLESPOONS MEDIUM CURRY PASTE

150ML (¼ PINT) COCONUT MILK

150ML (¼ PINT) VEGETABLE STOCK

1 x 420G (15OZ) CAN CHICKPEAS, DRAINED
    AND RINSED

225G (8OZ) LARGE PASTA SHELLS

225G (8OZ) FROZEN COOKED PRAWNS,
    THAWED

1 BUNCH FRESH CORIANDER, CHOPPED

SALT AND FRESHLY GROUND BLACK PEPPER

1. Heat the oil in a pan. Add the onion and fry for 5 minutes until softened. Add the curry paste and fry for 1 minute.

2. Stir in the coconut milk, vegetable stock and drained chickpeas. Bring to the boil and simmer for 10 minutes. Meanwhile, cook the pasta in a pan of boiling water as directed on the packet.

3. Stir the prawns into the chickpea curry and simmer for 2 minutes. Drain the pasta and divide between 2 serving dishes. Stir the chopped coriander into the prawn and chickpea curry, spoon over the pasta and serve at once.

THIS IS A WONDERFUL WAY OF SERVING CHICKPEAS WITH PASTA IN A RICH, LIGHTLY SPICED, COCONUT CURRY WITH PRAWNS. THE RESULT IS FULL OF FLAVOUR AND A PERFECT SUPPER DISH THAT CAN BE KNOCKED TOGETHER IN NO TIME!

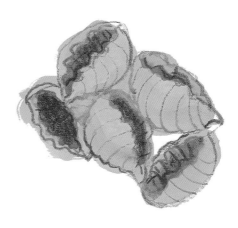

Green coconut broth with chicken & soba noodles

SERVES 4

2 TABLESPOONS SOY SAUCE

2 TABLESPOONS OLIVE OIL

JUICE AND GRATED RIND OF 1 LIME

2 CHICKEN BREASTS, EACH CUT INTO 6 STRIPS

1-2 TABLESPOONS GREEN THAI CURRY PASTE,
    TO TASTE

300ML (½ PINT) CHICKEN STOCK

1 x 400ML (14FL OZ) CAN COCONUT MILK

115G (4OZ) SHIITAKE MUSHROOMS, EACH CUT
    INTO 3 SLICES

300G (10½OZ) FRESH SOBA NOODLES

1 BUNCH FRESH CORIANDER, ROUGHLY CHOPPED

SALT

1. In a medium bowl, mix together the soy sauce, 1 tablespoon of the olive oil and the lime rind. Add the chicken pieces and set aside to marinate for 10-15 minutes.

2. Place a medium pan over the heat, add the curry paste and fry for 30 seconds. Add the chicken stock and coconut milk, bring to the boil and simmer for 5-6 minutes.

3. Heat ½ tablespoon of the oil in a large frying pan. Add the chicken with all of the marinade juices and stir-fry for 3 minutes. Add the remaining oil and the shiitake mushrooms and stir-fry for a further 2-3 minutes until golden.

4 Cook the soba noodles in a pan of boiling water as directed on the packet, then drain.

5. To serve, stir the lime juice into the coconut broth and season with salt. Ladle the broth into 4 dishes and pile some noodles into the centre of each. Spoon over the chicken and mushrooms, scatter over the coriander and serve at once.

SOBA NOODLES ARE MADE FROM BUCKWHEAT AND GIVE A DELICIOUS NUTTY FLAVOUR TO THIS SPICY BROTH.

Hot & sour prawn noodle soup

SERVES 4

1 TABLESPOON GROUNDNUT OIL

JUICE AND GRATED RIND OF 1 LIME

200G (7OZ) RAW TIGER PRAWNS, PEELED

1-2 TABLESPOONS RED THAI CURRY PASTE

1 x 400G (14OZ) CAN CHERRY TOMATOES

1 KAFFIR LIME LEAF, ROUGHLY CRUMBLED

200ML (7FL OZ) CHICKEN STOCK

2 TEASPOONS SUGAR

115G (4OZ) RICE NOODLES

1 BUNCH FRESH CORIANDER LEAVES

SALT AND FRESHLY GROUND BLACK PEPPER

1. Mix together the oil and half of the lime juice in a small bowl. Add the prawns and set aside to marinate.

2. Place a large saucepan over the heat, add the Thai curry paste and fry for 10 seconds. Add the canned tomatoes, lime leaf, stock, sugar, lime rind and remaining lime juice. Bring to the boil and simmer for 10-12 minutes. Season to taste.

3. Cook the noodles in a pan of boiling water as directed on the packet.

4. Heat a wok or large frying pan and add the marinated prawns. Stir-fry for 1-2 minutes or until the prawns are pink and cooked. Stir in the coriander leaves.

5. To serve, divide the hot and sour soup between 4 serving bowls. Pile in the noodles and arrange the prawns on the top. Serve at once.

YOU CAN BUY RED THAI CURRY PASTE FROM MOST SUPERMARKETS OR ORIENTAL STORES. DO TASTE TO CHECK THE HEAT AS THE PASTES CAN VARY QUITE CONSIDERABLY. COOKED PRAWNS CAN BE USED IN PLACE OF RAW ONES, BUT DO NOT ADD THEM UNTIL A MINUTE BEFORE SERVING OR THEY WILL BECOME HARD LIKE BULLETS!

Pad Thai noodles

SERVES 4

280G (10OZ) RICE NOODLES

3 TABLESPOONS LIGHT SOY SAUCE

2 TABLESPOONS FISH SAUCE

1 TABLESPOON TOMATO PURÉE

2 TABLESPOONS WATER

1 TEASPOON SUGAR

3 TABLESPOONS SUNFLOWER OIL

350G (12OZ) RAW TIGER PRAWNS, PEELED

2 CLOVES GARLIC, CRUSHED

2 RED CHILLIES, DESEEDED AND FINELY CHOPPED

1 BUNCH SPRING ONIONS, CHOPPED

3 EGGS, BEATEN

115G (4OZ) WHITE CRAB MEAT

140G (5OZ) BEAN SPROUTS

2 TABLESPOONS CASHEW NUTS, ROASTED

1 BUNCH FRESH CORIANDER, CHOPPED

LIME WEDGES, TO SERVE

1. Cook the noodles in a pan of boiling water as directed on the packet and drain. Run them under cold water and drain thoroughly. Set aside.

2. In a bowl, mix together the soy sauce, fish sauce, tomato purée, water and sugar. Set to one side.

3. Heat the oil in a large wok. Add the prawns and stir-fry for 1 minute. Add the garlic, chillies and spring onions and stir-fry for a further 2-3 minutes, or until the prawns are just cooked.

4. Push the prawns, garlic, chilli and spring onions to one side of the pan, and pour the eggs into the other side of the pan. Cook the egg over the heat, stirring constantly for 1 minute, or until the egg is just set.

5. Mix all the pan contents together, pour in the reserved soy sauce and tomato mixture and heat gently. Add the crab, bean sprouts, cooked rice noodles, cashew nuts and coriander. Toss everything together well and heat thoroughly.

6. To serve, pile the noodles into serving bowls and serve at once with the lime wedges.

SPICY NOODLES FROM THAILAND WITH EGGS, PRAWNS AND CASHEW NUTS MAKE A FILLING DISH. THIS IS EASIEST PILED INTO BOWLS FOR SERVING.

Moroccan macaroni

SERVES 4

1 TABLESPOON SUNFLOWER OR GRAPESEED OIL

1 ONION, CHOPPED

450G (1LB) LEAN MINCED LAMB

1 CLOVE GARLIC, CRUSHED

1 TEASPOON GROUND CARDAMOM

½ TEASPOON CINNAMON

2 TEASPOONS GROUND CORIANDER

2 TEASPOONS GROUND CUMIN

1 x 400G (14OZ) CAN CHOPPED TOMATOES IN
    TOMATO JUICE

300ML (½ PINT) VEGETABLE STOCK

175G (6OZ) SULTANAS

12 BLACK OLIVES, PITTED AND HALVED

225G (8OZ) QUICK-COOK BABY MACARONI

55G (2OZ) PINE NUTS, TOASTED

SALT AND FRESHLY GROUND BLACK PEPPER

1. Heat the oil in a large flameproof casserole. Add the chopped onion and fry for 5 minutes until softened. Add the minced lamb and fry over a medium heat for 3-4 minutes, until browned, then add the garlic and spices and fry for 1 minute.

2. Stir in the tomatoes and vegetable stock. Add the sultanas and olives and season well. Bring to the boil, cover and simmer for 15 minutes.

3. Meanwhile, preheat the oven to Gas Mark 6/200°C/400°F.

4. After 15 minutes, stir the quick-cook macaroni into the casserole. Cover again and transfer to the oven. Bake for 5 minutes, then remove the lid and bake for a further 10 minutes or until the pasta is cooked. Scatter with the toasted pine nuts and serve at once

THIS HEARTY DISH WITH SPICY LAMB AND FRUIT IS UNQUESTIONABLY MOROCCAN IN STYLE. SERVE IT WITH A CRISP GREEN SALAD AND CRUSTY BREAD.

Sichuan beef noodles

SERVES 4

1 TABLESPOON SICHUAN PEPPERCORNS,
    DRY-ROASTED AND LIGHTLY CRUSHED

3 TABLESPOONS DARK SOY SAUCE

2 TABLESPOONS RUNNY HONEY

2 TABLESPOONS GROUNDNUT OIL

2 x 140G (5OZ) SIRLOIN STEAKS, CUT
    LENGTHWAYS INTO THIN STRIPS

250G (9OZ) MEDIUM EGG NOODLES

1 BUNCH SPRING ONIONS, ROUGHLY CHOPPED

2 GREEN PEPPERS, CUT INTO THIN STRIPS

1 SMALL BUNCH FRESH CORIANDER, ROUGHLY
    CHOPPED

1. In a bowl, mix together the Sichuan peppercorns, soy sauce, honey and 1 tablespoon of the oil. Add the strips of steak and set aside to marinate.

2. Cook the egg noodles in a pan of boiling water as directed on the packet.

3. Meanwhile, heat the remaining oil in a large wok. Add the chopped spring onions and green peppers and stir-fry for 3-4 minutes, until slightly coloured. Add the marinated beef and cook for 2-3 minutes over a high heat.

4. To serve, drain the noodles, toss with the beef and chopped coriander and serve at once.

SICHUAN, OR SZECHUAN, PEPPERCORNS ARE CHINESE IN ORIGIN, AND REDDISH-BROWN IN COLOUR. BEFORE BEING ADDED TO A DISH, THEY SHOULD IDEALLY BE DRY-ROASTED IN A FRYING PAN AND THEN CRUSHED TO RELEASE THEIR FLAVOUR. BEEF OR PORK WORKS EQUALLY WELL IN THIS RECIPE.

Guacamole chillied pasta

SERVES 2-3

175G (6OZ) DRIED TOMATO AND CHILLI PASTA
CHOPPED FRESH CORIANDER, TO GARNISH

FOR THE GUACAMOLE RELISH

2 TABLESPOONS OLIVE OIL

225G (8OZ) BABY PLUM TOMATOES, COARSELY
    DICED

1 LARGE RIPE AVOCADO, STONED, PEELED AND
    COARSELY DICED

JUICE OF ½ LEMON

1 CLOVE GARLIC, CRUSHED

1 RED CHILLI, FINELY CHOPPED

½ RED ONION, FINELY CHOPPED

PINCH OF SUGAR

1 BUNCH FRESH CORIANDER, ROUGHLY CHOPPED

SALT AND FRESHLY GROUND BLACK PEPPER

1. Cook the tomato and chilli pasta in a pan of boiling water as directed on the packet and drain well.

2. Meanwhile, combine all the relish ingredients together in a bowl, reserving half of the chopped coriander, and season well.

3. To serve, toss the hot pasta with the guacamole relish. Pile into 2 or 3 serving bowls and scatter with the remaining coriander. Grind over a little more black pepper and serve at once.

Spanish chorizo & olive

SERVES 4

1 TABLESPOON OLIVE OIL

1 ONION, CHOPPED

1 HEAPED TEASPOON TURMERIC

250G (9OZ) TINY DRIED PASTA TWISTS

600ML (1 PINT) VEGETABLE STOCK

1 HEAPED TEASPOON DRIED HERBES DE
   PROVENCE

225G (8OZ) CHORIZO SAUSAGE, DICED

24 BLACK AND GREEN OLIVES, PITTED AND
   HALVED

1. Heat the oil in a large pan. Add the onion and fry for 5 minutes until softened. Stir in the turmeric and fry for 1 minute.

2. Stir in the pasta, stock and herbes de Provence. Season well and bring to the boil, then cover and cook for 4 minutes.

3. Stir in the diced chorizo and the olives and cook, uncovered, for a further 4-5 minutes, or until the pasta is cooked. Add a little water if the mixture becomes too dry.

CHORIZO SAUSAGE AND GLISTENING OLIVES ARE COMBINED WITH TINY PASTA TWISTS IN THIS LIGHTLY SPICED SPANISH-STYLE DISH.

Crab noodle soup

SERVES 4

850ML (1½ PINTS) CHICKEN STOCK

150ML (¼ PINT) WHITE WINE

1 RED CHILLI, CHOPPED OR 1 TEASPOON CHILLI
   SAUCE

1 BAY LEAF

115G (4OZ) THREAD EGG NOODLES

1 x 198G (7OZ) CAN CREAMED SWEETCORN

1 x 170G (5¾ OZ) CAN CRAB MEAT, DRAINED
   AND FLAKED

SALT AND FRESHLY GROUND BLACK PEPPER

4 TABLESPOONS CHOPPED FRESH FLAT-LEAF
   PARSLEY

LIME WEDGES, TO SERVE

1. Heat the stock in a large pan. Add the wine, chilli and bay leaf. Bring to the boil and simmer for 5 minutes.

2. Add the noodles and simmer for 3 minutes until cooked. Stir in the creamed sweetcorn and crab meat, season and simmer for a further 1 minute.

3. To serve, spoon into bowls and scatter with the chopped parsley. Squeeze a little of the juice from the lime wedges into each bowl and serve at once.

A CHINESE-INSPIRED SOUP WITH THREAD EGG NOODLES, WHICH IS VERY DIFFICULT NOT TO SLURP AND IDEAL FOR LUNCH!

2 Modern classics

Classic dishes like spaghetti bolognaise and lasagne were once at the forefront of Italian food outside Italy, yet these days they are often discounted as being old-fashioned and dull. This chapter is dedicated to reviving these pasta classics. A tuck here and a tweak there strip away the years to reveal superb dishes that have stood the test of time and can still delight today.

Old favourites are revisited in a lighter, more modern manner. By substituting one ingredient for another, the authenticity may be lost, but the flavour wins. And what's more, you'll find these recipes quick and simple to make.

Macaroni cheese with sage & prosciutto

SERVES 4

280G (10OZ) DRIED MACARONI

85G (3OZ) PARMA HAM, TORN INTO STRIPS

1 BUNCH FRESH SAGE, CHOPPED

40G (1½OZ) FRESH BREADCRUMBS

CRISP SALAD LEAVES, TO SERVE

FOR THE SAUCE

425ML (¾ PINT) WHITE WINE

300ML (½ PINT) VEGETABLE STOCK

1 BAY LEAF

115G (4OZ) MATURE CHEDDAR CHEESE, GRATED

115G (4OZ) GRUYÈRE CHEESE, GRATED

2 TABLESPOONS BRANDY

1 ½ TABLESPOONS CORNFLOUR

SALT AND FRESHLY GROUND BLACK PEPPER

1. Cook the macaroni in a pan of boiling water as directed on the packet. Drain and set aside.

2. Preheat the oven to Gas Mark 6/200°C/400°F.

4. To make the sauce, simmer together the wine and stock in a pan with the bay leaf for 10 minutes. Add three-quarters of the grated Cheddar and Gruyère and stir over a low heat until melted. Mix the brandy with the cornflour in a cup then add to the sauce. Season and simmer for 1-2 minutes.

5. Toss the macaroni, Parma ham and chopped sage together and transfer to a large, shallow ovenproof dish. Pour over the hot sauce. Combine the remaining cheese with the breadcrumbs and scatter over the dish.

4 Bake in the oven for 15-20 minutes until golden. Serve hot or cold with crisp salad leaves.

Fettuccine with cream & lemon

SERVES 4

300ML (½ PINT) DOUBLE CREAM

GRATED RIND OF 2 LEMONS

2 TEASPOONS LEMON JUICE

450G (1LB) FRESH FETTUCCINE OR TAGLIATELLE

55G (2OZ) PECORINO CHEESE, GRATED

2 TABLESPOONS CHOPPED FRESH FLAT-LEAF
   PARSLEY

SALT AND FRESHLY GROUND BLACK PEPPER

1. Pour the cream into a saucepan. Add the grated lemon rind and season well with plenty of black pepper and salt. Bring to the boil over a low heat and simmer gently for 5-6 minutes. Remove from the heat and stir in the lemon juice.

2. Meanwhile, cook the fettuccine in a pan of boiling water as directed on the packet.

3. To serve, drain the fettuccine and return to the pan. Add the lemon sauce, grated cheese and chopped parsley. Toss together briefly and serve at once.

I HAD THIS DISH IN ROME FOR LUNCH - SO SIMPLE, YET REALLY FABULOUS! IT IS A DELICIOUSLY RICH DISH THAT WILL SERVE 4 AS A MAIN COURSE, OR 6 AS A STARTER. FOLLOW WITH A CRISP REFRESHING SALAD FOR A PERFECT LUNCH.

Fresh tomato pasta

SERVES 4

900G (2LB) TASTY TOMATOES (ON THE VINE OR CHERRY), ROUGHLY CHOPPED

2½ TABLESPOONS VIRGIN OLIVE OIL

1 CLOVE GARLIC, CRUSHED

1-2 RED CHILLIES, DESEEDED AND ROUGHLY CHOPPED

PINCH OF SUGAR

LARGE HANDFUL FRESH BASIL LEAVES, TORN

SALT AND FRESHLY GROUND BLACK PEPPER

450G (1LB) FRESH PASTA OR SPINACH AND RICOTTA-STUFFED TORTELLINI OR RAVIOLI

1. Place the chopped tomatoes in a food processor and process briefly to break up. Do not overprocess or they will become frothy. Set aside.

2. Heat ½ tablespoon of the oil in a large pan. Add the garlic and chillies and fry gently for 1 minute. Add the tomatoes and the sugar to the pan and heat gently. As soon as the sauce is hot, remove immediately from the heat. Stir in the basil and remaining virgin olive oil and season to taste.

3. Meanwhile, cook your chosen pasta in a pan of boiling water as directed on the packet and drain well.

4. To serve, arrange the pasta in individual serving bowls and spoon over the fresh tomato vinaigrette or, if using tortellini, spoon a pool of sauce on to each plate, top with a pile of stuffed tortellini and a sprinkling of ground black pepper.

THIS CHUNKY VINAIGRETTE REQUIRES THE FRESHEST, TASTIEST TOMATOES YOU CAN FIND.

Lasagne

SERVES 4

6 SHEETS FRESH LASAGNE

FOR THE MEAT SAUCE

½ TABLESPOON OLIVE OIL

1 LARGE ONION, CHOPPED

450G (1LB) GOOD-QUALITY MINCED BEEF

1 CLOVE GARLIC, CRUSHED

2 TABLESPOONS CHOPPED FRESH OREGANO

1 x 400G (14OZ) CAN CHOPPED TOMATOES IN
    TOMATO JUICE

1 TABLESPOON SUN-DRIED TOMATO PASTE

150ML (¼ PINT) RED WINE

SALT AND FRESHLY GROUND BLACK PEPPER

FOR THE CHEESE SAUCE

300ML (½ PINT) DOUBLE CREAM

85G (3OZ) PARMESAN CHEESE, GRATED

LARGE PINCH OF NUTMEG

SALT AND FRESHLY GROUND BLACK PEPPER

1. To make the meat sauce, heat the oil in a large pan. Add the chopped onion and fry for 5 minutes. Add the mince and garlic and fry for a further 3-4 minutes until the mince is lightly browned.

2. Stir in the oregano, canned tomatoes, tomato paste and red wine. Season well, cover and simmer for 30 minutes. Remove the lid and simmer for a further 10 minutes.

3. Meanwhile, preheat the oven to Gas Mark 4/180°C/350°F. Soak the lasagne sheets as directed on the packet. In a bowl, combine the cream and three-quarters of the Parmesan cheese. Season well with nutmeg, salt and pepper to taste.

4. Pour half the cooked meat sauce into the base of a large ovenproof dish. Cover with 3 sheets of lasagne. Pour over the remaining meat sauce and top with the remaining lasagne. Pour over the cheese sauce and scatter over the remaining Parmesan cheese. Transfer the lasagne to the oven for 30 minutes until browned and bubbling hot.

HERE'S A LASAGNE THAT'S NOT HARD WORK! RATHER THAN THE TRADITIONAL ROUX-BASED WHITE SAUCE, CREATING YET ANOTHER DIRTY PAN, THE WHITE SAUCE IS QUITE SIMPLY A SERIOUSLY GENEROUS CONCOCTION OF PARMESAN CHEESE, NUTMEG AND DOUBLE CREAM.

Cod cassoulet

SERVES 4

1 TABLESPOON OLIVE OIL

1 LARGE ONION, CHOPPED

4 RASHERS SMOKED LEAN BACON, CHOPPED

4 x 115G (4OZ) SKINLESS, BONELESS CHUNKY
    COD FILLETS

4 LARGE LETTUCE LEAVES

150ML (¼ PINT) WHITE WINE

1 BUNCH FRESH TARRAGON, CHOPPED

225G (8OZ) FRESH PENNE

300ML (½ PINT) VEGETABLE STOCK

SALT AND FRESHLY GROUND BLACK PEPPER

225G (8OZ) FRESH PEAS

150ML (¼ PINT) DOUBLE CREAM

FOR THE TOPPING

½ TABLESPOON OLIVE OIL

4 TABLESPOONS FRESH BREADCRUMBS

25G (1OZ) GRUYÈRE CHEESE, GRATED

2 TABLESPOONS ROUGHLY CHOPPED FRESH
    PARSLEY

1. Heat the oil in a large shallow frying pan. Add the chopped onion and bacon and fry for 5 minutes, until softened and golden.

2. Wrap each piece of cod in a lettuce leaf and lay in the pan. Pour in the white wine, sprinkle in the tarragon and simmer for 1 minute. Place the pasta around the fish, pour the vegetable stock over the pasta and season. Bring to the boil, cover and simmer for 5 minutes. Then remove the lid and add the peas and cream. Simmer, uncovered, for a further 2 minutes, or until the fish and pasta are cooked.

3. Meanwhile, preheat the grill to its highest setting and mix all the topping ingredients together in a bowl. When the pasta is cooked, scatter over the topping. Place the pan under the grill for a few minutes until the topping is crisp and golden.

CASSOULETS ARE USUALLY BASED ON BEANS, FLAVOURED WITH PORK AND GOOSE FAT. TRY THIS FISHY, SIMPLER VERSION, USING FRESH PEAS, BACON, COD AND, OF COURSE, PASTA!

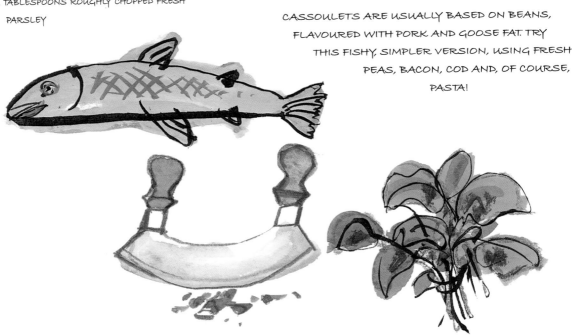

Wild stroganoff

SERVES 4

55G (2OZ) UNSALTED BUTTER

1 LARGE RED ONION, THINLY SLICED

225G (8OZ) MIXED WILD MUSHROOMS

350G (12OZ) DRIED PAPPARDELLE

450G (1LB) SIRLOIN STEAK, FAT REMOVED AND
     CUT INTO THIN STRIPS

CRACKED BLACK PEPPER

2 TABLESPOONS BRANDY

3 TABLESPOONS CRÈME FRAÎCHE

1 BUNCH FRESH FLAT-LEAF PARSLEY, CHOPPED

1. Heat half of the butter in a large frying pan. Add the red onion and fry for 5 minutes until softened. Add the mushrooms and fry for a further 4-5 minutes until cooked. Remove the onions and mushrooms from the pan and keep warm.

2. Cook the pappardelle in a pan of boiling water as directed on the packet.

3. Season the steak well with cracked black pepper.

4. Heat the remaining butter in the pan until very hot, but not burning. Add the strips of steak to the pan, pour over the brandy and ignite. Fry the beef over a high heat for 2-3 minutes, or until it is done to your liking. Return the onion and mushrooms to the pan, add the crème fraîche and bring the sauce to the boil.

5. To serve, drain the pasta and toss with the chopped parsley. Transfer to serving plates and immediately spoon over the hot stroganoff. Serve at once.

HERE WE'VE RESURRECTED A POPULAR SEVENTIES DISH AND GIVEN IT A MODERN TOUCH. NOTE THAT PORK MAKES A GOOD ALTERNATIVE TO THE BEEF USED HERE.

Roast Greek vegetable pasta

SERVES 4

250G (9OZ) BABY AUBERGINES, CUT IN HALF
   LENGTHWAYS
2 RED ONIONS, EACH CUT INTO 6 WEDGES
3 CLOVES GARLIC, UNPEELED
1 SPRIG OF ROSEMARY
2 TABLESPOONS OLIVE OIL
SALT AND FRESHLY GROUND BLACK PEPPER
280G (10OZ) CHERRY TOMATOES
225G (8OZ) FRESH SPAGHETTI

FOR THE DRESSING

175G (6OZ) FETA CHEESE, CRUMBLED
12 GREEK-STYLE BLACK OLIVES, PITTED AND
   ROUGHLY CHOPPED
2 TABLESPOONS VIRGIN OLIVE OIL
1 BUNCH FRESH FLAT-LEAF PARSLEY, ROUGHLY
   CHOPPED
JUICE OF 1 LEMON

1. Preheat the oven to Gas Mark 6/200°C/400°F.

2. Place the aubergines, onions, garlic and rosemary in a roasting tin. Drizzle over the oil and season well. Transfer to the oven and roast for 30 minutes, turning the vegetables halfway through cooking.

3. Add the cherry tomatoes to the roasted vegetables and roast for a further 15 minutes, until they are golden and tender.

4. To make the dressing, toss together the feta, olives, olive oil and parsley in a bowl. Season well with black pepper and lemon juice to taste.

5. Cook the spaghetti in a pan of boiling water as directed on the packet.

6. To serve, drain the spaghetti and toss with the dressing. Transfer to a large serving platter and pile on the roasted vegetables. Serve at once with warm crusty bread.

CRUMBLY FETA, BAKED AUBERGINE, OLIVES AND LEMON - HERE IS A CLASSIC TASTE OF THE MEDITERRANEAN

Thin courgette lasagne

SERVES 4
675G (1½LB) PLUM TOMATOES, THICKLY SLICED
SALT AND FRESHLY GROUND BLACK PEPPER
1 TABLESPOON OLIVE OIL
½ TABLESPOON BALSAMIC VINEGAR
425ML (¾ PINT) DOUBLE CREAM
115G (4OZ) GRUYÈRE CHEESE, FINELY GRATED
450G (1LB) COURGETTES
8 SHEETS FRESH EGG LASAGNE
2 TABLESPOONS CHOPPED FRESH PARSLEY

1. Preheat the oven to Gas Mark 6/200°C/400°F.

2. Lightly grease a large ovenproof dish. Stack the tomato slices in the bottom of the dish, seasoning each layer with salt and pepper and drizzling over a little oil and balsamic vinegar. Place the dish in the oven and roast the tomatoes for 30 minutes.

3. Meanwhile, combine the cream and 85g (3oz) of the grated cheese in a bowl. Season and set to one side. Cut the courgettes lengthways, into long thin slices and soak the lasagne sheets as directed on the packet.

4. Remove the roasted tomatoes from the oven and top with 4 sheets of the lasagne. Spoon over half the cream and cheese mixture and top with a layer of courgette slices. Season well. Top with 4 more lasagne sheets, the remaining cream and cheese mixture and another layer of courgettes. Season again. Finally, scatter over the remaining Gruyère and the chopped parsley. Return to the oven and bake for a further 25-30 minutes, until bubbling and golden.

A SCRUMPTIOUS VEGETABLE VERSION OF THE FAMOUS CLASSIC.

Spaghetti with meatballs

SERVES 4

350G (12OZ) DRIED SPAGHETTI

1 QUANTITY RED HOT TOMATO SAUCE (SEE PAGE 80)

55G (2OZ) PARMESAN CHEESE, GRATED

FOR THE MEATBALLS

450G (1LB) LEAN MINCED PORK

115G (4OZ) FRESH WHITE BREADCRUMBS

1 LARGE ONION, VERY FINELY CHOPPED

1 EGG, BEATEN

1 TABLESPOON SUN-DRIED TOMATO PASTE

2 TABLESPOONS CHOPPED FRESH PARSLEY

1 TABLESPOON CHOPPED FRESH OREGANO

SALT AND FRESHLY GROUND BLACK PEPPER

1. Preheat the oven to Gas Mark 6/200°C/400°F and lightly grease a large roasting tin or baking tray.

2. Place all the meatball ingredients in a food processor. Season well and blend together. Form the mixture into about 18 balls, roughly golf ball-sized, and place them in the prepared roasting tin. Roast the meatballs for 25-30 minutes, until browned and cooked.

3. When the meatballs are nearly cooked, cook the spaghetti in a pan of boiling water as directed on the packet and heat the red hot tomato sauce. Drain the cooked spaghetti and toss with the grated Parmesan. Season with black pepper.

4. To serve, divide the spaghetti between 4 serving plates. Top each with 4 or 5 meatballs and spoon over the red hot tomato sauce.

ROASTING THE MEATBALLS IN THE OVEN RATHER THAN IN THE SAUCE RIDS THEM OF EXCESS FAT AND MAKES FOR A CLEAN, SPICY ACCOMPANYING SAUCE

Spaghetti with clams

SERVES 4

36 SMALL CLAMS

450G (1LB) DRIED SPAGHETTI OR LINGUINI

1 TABLESPOON OLIVE OIL

2 CLOVES GARLIC, CRUSHED

150ML (¼ PINT) WHITE WINE

40G (1½OZ) BUTTER

1 BUNCH FRESH FLAT-LEAF PARSLEY, CHOPPED

SALT AND FRESHLY GROUND BLACK PEPPER

1. Scrub and wash the clams well. Discard any that are cracked or remain open when tapped.

2. Cook the spaghetti or linguini in a pan of boiling water, as directed on the packet.

3. Meanwhile, heat the olive oil in a pan. Add the crushed garlic and cook gently for 20 seconds. Add the clams and white wine and cover. Simmer for 4-5 minutes until the clams have opened.

4. Strain the clams, discarding any that have not opened, and reserve the cooking liquid. Return this liquid to the pan. Place the pan over a high heat and boil until the clam liquid is reduced by half. Remove from the heat and stir in the butter, chopped parsley and clams.

5. Drain the spaghetti and toss it briefly but thoroughly with the clam sauce. Season and serve at once.

Leek cannelloni

SERVES 4

4 THIN LEEKS, WASHED AND HALVED WIDTHWAYS

8 DRIED CANNELLONI TUBES

1 QUANTITY RED HOT TOMATO SAUCE (SEE PAGE 80)

225G (8OZ) FETA CHEESE, CRUMBLED

SALAD LEAVES, TO SERVE

1. Preheat the oven to Gas Mark 6/200°C/400°F.

2. Simmer the leeks in a pan of boiling water for 5 minutes.

3. Lightly butter a shallow ovenproof dish. Drain the leeks and push each half through a cannelloni tube. Lay the stuffed cannelloni side by side in the dish.

4. Gently heat the hot tomato sauce before pouring it over the cannelloni. Scatter over the feta cheese.

5. Bake in the oven for 40-45 minutes, until bubbling hot. Serve at once on a bed of crisp salad leaves.

THIS DISH OF TASTY SWEET LEEKS, ENCASED IN PASTA, BAKED IN A RICH TOMATO SAUCE AND TOPPED WITH FETA, IS IDEAL FOR A TASTY LUNCH.

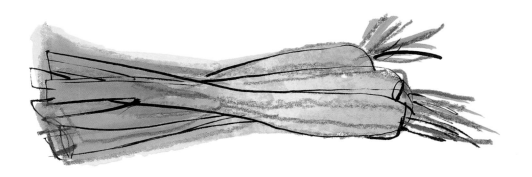

Spaghetti bolognaise

SERVES 3-4

115G (4OZ) DRIED OR FRESH SPAGHETTI
   PER PERSON

1 TEASPOON OLIVE OIL

FRESH PARMESAN CHEESE SHAVINGS

FOR THE MEAT SAUCE

½ TABLESPOON OLIVE OIL

1 LARGE ONION, CHOPPED

450G (1LB) GOOD-QUALITY MINCED BEEF

1 CLOVE GARLIC, CRUSHED

2 TABLESPOONS CHOPPED FRESH OREGANO

1 X 400G (14OZ) CAN CHOPPED TOMATOES IN
   TOMATO JUICE

1 TABLESPOON SUN-DRIED TOMATO PASTE

150ML (¼ PINT) RED WINE

SALT AND FRESHLY GROUND BLACK PEPPER

1. To make the sauce, heat the oil in a large pan. Add the chopped onion and fry for 5 minutes. Add the mince and garlic and fry for a further 3-4 minutes, until the mince is lightly browned.

2. Stir in the chopped oregano, canned tomatoes, tomato paste and red wine. Season well. Cover and simmer for 45 minutes, adding a little extra wine if the sauce becomes too dry.

3. Just before the sauce is cooked, cook the spaghetti in a pan of boiling water as directed on the packet. Drain well and toss with the olive oil. Arrange the spaghetti on 3 or 4 individual serving plates and spoon some sauce into the centre of each. Scatter over the shavings of Parmesan and serve at once.

SPAGHETTI WILL ALWAYS BE THE PERFECT PASTA FOR THIS CLASSIC MEAT SAUCE. RICH SUN-DRIED TOMATO PASTE IS USED IN PLACE OF THE NORMAL TOMATO PURÉE AND FRESH OREGANO RATHER THAN DRIED GIVES THIS CLASSIC A SIMPLE BUT EFFECTIVE MAKEOVER.

Spaghetti alla carbonara

SERVES 2
175G (6OZ) DRIED SPAGHETTI
2 LARGE EGGS
2 TABLESPOONS CRÈME FRAÎCHE
SALT AND FRESHLY GROUND BLACK PEPPER
55G (2OZ) SPINACH, FINELY SHREDDED
4 RASHERS SMOKED BACK BACON, CUT INTO
   STRIPS
25G (1OZ) PARMESAN CHEESE, GRATED

1. Cook the spaghetti in a pan of boiling water as directed on the packet.

2. Meanwhile, combine the eggs and crème fraîche in a bowl and season well. Stir in the spinach.

3. Dry-fry the strips of bacon in a large pan for 5 minutes until cooked. Drain the cooked spaghetti and add to the hot bacon pan. Pour in the egg and spinach mixture, stir immediately and remove from the heat. Do not allow the egg to curdle.

4. Serve at once, sprinkled with the Parmesan.

THE ADDITIONS OF FRESH SPINACH AND CRÈME FRAÎCHE TO THIS FAVOURITE CLASSIC RECIPE REALLY GIVE IT A LIGHTER, MODERN TASTE.

Bagnacauda

SERVES 4
2 X 50G (2OZ) CANS ANCHOVIES, DRAINED
85ML (3FL OZ) MILK
150ML (¼ PINT) VIRGIN OLIVE OIL
6 CLOVES GARLIC, CRUSHED
300ML (½ PINT) WHITE WINE
SQUEEZE OF LEMON JUICE
FRESHLY GROUND BLACK PEPPER
450G (1LB) FRESH PASTA, COOKED

1. In a bowl, soak the anchovies in the milk for 30 minutes. Then transfer the anchovies to a small food processor with 2 tablespoons of the milk and process to a smooth paste. Set aside.

2. Heat 1 tablespoon of the oil in a pan and add the crushed garlic. Gently fry for 2-3 minutes, being careful not to let the garlic burn. Add the white wine and simmer until the liquid has reduced by half.

3. Stir in the reserved anchovy paste and the remaining olive oil and heat gently. Season with lemon juice and freshly ground black pepper and serve at once tossed with freshly cooked pasta.

THIS IS NOT AN AUTHENTIC VERSION OF BAGNACAUDA BUT IS EQUALLY DELICIOUS. SERVE STRAIGHT FROM THE PAN AS A HOT DIP OR AS A SIMPLE DRESSING OVER PASTA.

3 Everyday Eating

Eating good food every day doesn't have to be expensive, time consuming or dull. The recipes in this chapter are ideal for family meals and many can be made with ordinary items found in your storecupboard, with or without the addition of a fresh ingredient or two. These days, the 'storecupboard' includes your freezer and fridge, as well as your larder. Your storecupboards don't have to be vast, just organized and user friendly. Keeping them well stocked will enable you to be truly spontaneous with your pasta. Next time you go shopping, take the time to buy a few special extras ready for delicious pasta meals at the drop of a hat. So don't just wait for a special occasion - try a new pasta dish any day of the week.

Peppered mackerel fillets with lime butter pasta

SERVES 4

40G (1½ OZ) UNSALTED BUTTER

1 SHALLOT, FINELY CHOPPED

150ML (¼ PINT) WHITE WINE

300ML (½ PINT) DOUBLE CREAM

JUICE OF 1 LIME

FRESHLY GROUND BLACK PEPPER

4 PEPPERED, SMOKED MACKEREL FILLETS

450G (1LB) FRESH LINGUINI

LIME WEDGES, TO SERVE

1. Preheat the grill to a medium setting.

2. Heat 15g (½oz) of the butter in a saucepan and gently fry the shallot for 5 minutes. Add the white wine and simmer until reduced by half. Stir in the double cream and simmer for 5 minutes. Stir in the remaining butter and the lime juice and season with black pepper.

3. Meanwhile, place the mackerel fillets under the grill for 5 minutes until lightly crisped and warmed through. Remove the skin and roughly flake the fish. Cook the pasta in a pan of boiling water as directed on the packet.

4. To serve, drain the pasta and toss with the flaked mackerel and the lime butter sauce. Pile into a large serving dish and serve at once with extra lime wedges.

THE LIME GIVES THIS DISH A REAL TASTY KICK. IT IS GOOD SERVED WITH UNDRESSED, CRISP, GREEN SALAD LEAVES.

Seafood pasta

SERVES 2-3

1 TABLESPOON GRAPESEED OR SUNFLOWER OIL

1 LARGE ONION, FINELY CHOPPED

1 CLOVE GARLIC, CRUSHED

1 x 400G (14OZ) CAN CHOPPED TOMATOES IN
  TOMATO JUICE

150ML (¼ PINT) RED WINE

SALT AND FRESHLY GROUND BLACK PEPPER

225G (8OZ) DRIED PENNE, TWISTS OR
  RIGATONI

1 x 185G (6½OZ) CAN TUNA IN OIL, DRAINED

1 x 85G (3OZ) CAN SMOKED MUSSELS OR
  OYSTERS, DRAINED

15 GREEN OLIVES, PITTED AND CHOPPED

1. Heat the oil in a pan. Add the onion and garlic and fry for 5 minutes until softened. Stir in the canned tomatoes and red wine and season. Bring to the boil, reduce the heat and simmer for 30 minutes, stirring occasionally.

2. When the sauce is ready, cook the pasta in a pan of boiling water as directed on the packet.

3. Drain and toss the hot pasta with the drained tuna, smoked mussels or oysters and chopped olives. Pile the hot pasta into 2 or 3 individual serving dishes and spoon over the rich tomato sauce.

YOU CAN BUY CANNED SMOKED OYSTERS OR MUSSELS FROM MOST LARGE SUPERMARKETS - THEY HAVE A REALLY DELICIOUS TEXTURE AND TASTE. IF YOU CANNOT FIND THEM, TRY USING FLAKES OF SMOKED TROUT OR PEPPERED SMOKED MACKEREL.

Chunky country pasta

SERVES 4

1 TABLESPOON OLIVE OIL

1 LARGE ONION, THICKLY SLICED

4 LARGE RASHERS SMOKED BACK BACON, CHOPPED

3 TABLESPOONS ROUGHLY CHOPPED FRESH OREGANO

1 BAY LEAF

15G (½OZ) SUN-DRIED RED PEPPERS, CHOPPED

1 LARGE CLOVE GARLIC, CRUSHED

1 COX APPLE, CORED AND FINELY SLICED

150ML (¼ PINT) WHITE WINE

600-900ML (1-1½ PINTS) VEGETABLE STOCK

350G (12OZ) DRIED PENNE

115G (4OZ) SPRING GREENS, FINELY SHREDDED

55G (2OZ) PARMESAN CHEESE, GRATED

SALT AND FRESHLY GROUND BLACK PEPPER

1. Heat the oil in a large pan or wok. Add the onion and bacon and fry for 5 minutes. Stir in the oregano, bay leaf, sun-dried peppers, garlic, apple, white wine and 600ml (1 pint) of the stock. Bring to the boil, cover and simmer for 5 minutes.

2. Add the penne and season. Cover again and simmer for a further 10-12 minutes, or until the pasta is cooked, adding more stock if the mixture becomes too dry. Stir in the spring greens.

3. To serve, stir through the grated Parmesan and serve at once.

IF YOU ARE VERY HUNGRY, GARLIC CROÛTES WOULD MAKE A DELICIOUS ACCOMPANIMENT TO THIS HEARTY DINNER. TO MAKE THEM, SIMPLY RUB A CLOVE OF GARLIC OVER THICK SLICES OF COUNTRY BREAD AND TOAST UNDER THE GRILL.

Smoky bacon lentils with pasta

SERVES 4

1 TABLESPOON OLIVE OIL

2 LEEKS, SHREDDED

6 RASHERS SMOKED BACON, CHOPPED

2 CLOVES GARLIC, CRUSHED

200G (7OZ) ORANGE LENTILS

150ML (¼ PINT) WHITE WINE

900ML (1½ PINTS) VEGETABLE STOCK

1 BAY LEAF

140G (5OZ) DRIED PASTA SHELLS

JUICE OF ½ LEMON

SALT AND FRESHLY GROUND BLACK PEPPER

GRATED RIND OF 1 LEMON

1 BUNCH FRESH CHIVES, CHOPPED

1. Heat the oil in a large pan. Add the shredded leeks and chopped bacon and fry for 5 minutes.

2. Add the garlic and lentils and stir in the white wine, vegetable stock and bay leaf. Bring to the boil and cook for 1 minute. Add the pasta shells, reduce the heat and simmer for a further 12 minutes, or until the lentils and pasta are cooked.

3. To serve, transfer the pasta to a large serving dish and sprinkle over the lemon juice. Season well and scatter with the lemon rind and chopped chives and serve at once.

THIS GUTSY BACON AND LENTIL DISH MAKES A TASTY WELCOMING MEAL. SERVE WITH CRUSTY GARLIC BREAD.

Red salmon kedgeree with mango chutney

SERVES 4

55G (2OZ) BUTTER

1 BUNCH SPRING ONIONS, CHOPPED

1 TABLESPOON GARAM MASALA

3 TABLESPOONS DRY SHERRY

JUICE OF 1 LEMON

55G (2OZ) SULTANAS

1 x 418G (14½OZ) CAN RED SALMON, DRAINED
   WITH THE JUICE RESERVED AND MADE UP TO
   600ML (1 PINT) WITH VEGETABLE STOCK

450G (1LB) FRESH PENNE

½ BUNCH FRESH DILL, CHOPPED

SALT AND FRESHLY GROUND BLACK PEPPER

3 EGGS, HARD-BOILED AND ROUGHLY CHOPPED

MANGO CHUTNEY, TO SERVE

LEMON WEDGES, TO SERVE

1. Melt the butter in a large frying pan or wok, add the spring onions and stir-fry for 30 seconds. Add the garam masala, sherry, lemon juice, sultanas and salmon juice and stock. Bring to the boil and simmer for 3 minutes.

2. Stir in the pasta, cover and simmer for 5-6 minutes until the pasta is cooked, adding a little extra water if the pan becomes too dry.

3. Roughly flake the salmon and fold it into the cooked pasta with the chopped dill. Season to taste and heat through until piping hot. Scatter with the chopped egg and serve at once, accompanied by mango chutney and lemon wedges.

KEDGEREE IS A FAMOUS VICTORIAN BREAKFAST DISH, ADAPTED FROM AN INDIAN DISH OF RICE, FISH AND CURRY. HERE IS ANOTHER VARIATION, USING PENNE IN PLACE OF THE RICE.

Sage & onion pasta bake

SERVES 4-6

1 TABLESPOON OLIVE OIL

1 LARGE ONION, CHOPPED

6 RASHERS SMOKED BACK BACON, DICED

2 SLICES WHITE BREAD, CUT INTO CUBES

175G (6OZ) DRIED CONCHIGLIETTE (TINY PASTA
SHELLS) OR RISI

425ML (¾ PINT) CHICKEN STOCK

150ML (¼ PINT) WHITE WINE

1 LARGE CARROT, GRATED

2 TABLESPOONS CHOPPED FRESH SAGE LEAVES

SALT AND FRESHLY GROUND BLACK PEPPER

1. Preheat the oven to Gas Mark 6/200°C/400°F.

2. Heat the oil in a large flameproof casserole. Add the onion, bacon and cubes of bread and fry for 5 minutes.

3. Stir in the pasta, chicken stock, white wine, grated carrot and sage and season well. Bring to the boil, cover and transfer to the oven for 15 minutes.

4. After 15 minutes, stir the mixture and return to the oven, to cook, uncovered, for a further 15-20 minutes, until lightly crisped.

I'M NOT A BIG FAN OF DRIED SAGE, BUT FRESH SAGE IS SOMETHING ELSE! USED FREQUENTLY IN ITALIAN COOKING, IT'S A HERB THAT DESERVES FAR MORE USE. THIS IS A TASTY DISH ON ITS OWN OR SERVE IT AS A DELICIOUS ACCOMPANIMENT TO TRADITIONAL ROAST CHICKEN.

Cheese & onion pasta

SERVES 2-3

2 LARGE RED ONIONS, CUT INTO WEDGES

1 TABLESPOON OLIVE OIL

225G (8OZ) DRIED RIGATONI

55G (2OZ) STILTON CHEESE, CRUMBLED

2 LARGE CELERY STICKS WITH LEAVES, FINELY
CHOPPED AND THE LEAVES RESERVED

1 TEASPOON WALNUT OIL (OPTIONAL)

SALT AND FRESHLY GROUND BLACK PEPPER

1. Preheat the grill to a low-medium setting.

2. Place the onion wedges on a baking tray and brush with the olive oil. Grill the onion wedges for 20-30 minutes, until softened and lightly charred.

3. Meanwhile, cook the pasta in a pan of boiling water as directed on the packet.

4. To serve, drain the pasta and toss with the Stilton, chopped celery, walnut oil, if using, and season. Stir through the grilled onion wedges, garnish with the celery leaves and serve at once.

THIS IS GREAT SERVED HOT OR COLD. TRY IT WITH GRILLED SAUSAGES IN PLACE OF THE USUAL MASHED POTATOES.

Clear chicken soup with basil pistou

SERVES 2-3

600ML (1 PINT) FRESH CHICKEN STOCK

150ML (¼ PINT) WHITE WINE

1 BAY LEAF

55G (2OZ) DRIED CONCHIGLIETTE (TINY PASTA
SHELLS) OR RISI

5G (⅛OZ) DRIED PORCINI MUSHROOMS, SOAKED
AND CUT INTO THIN STRIPS

1 CHICKEN BREAST, CUT INTO THIN STRIPS

2 SPRING ONIONS, HALVED AND CUT INTO THIN
STRIPS LENGTHWAYS

FOR THE PISTOU

2 TABLESPOONS FRESH BASIL LEAVES

2 TABLESPOONS CHOPPED FRESH FLAT-LEAF
PARSLEY

75ML (2½FL OZ) OLIVE OIL

½ TEASPOON LEMON RIND

SQUEEZE OF LEMON JUICE

PINCH OF CRUSHED GARLIC

SALT AND FRESHLY GROUND BLACK PEPPER

1. Simmer together the stock, wine and bay leaf in a large pan for 10 minutes.

2. Add the pasta shapes and porcini, and season. Simmer for a further 5 minutes, then add the strips of chicken and spring onion and simmer for a further 3 minutes, or until the chicken and pasta are cooked.

3. Meanwhile, blend all the pistou ingredients together in a small food processor.

4. To serve, ladle the soup into large shallow bowls. Drizzle each with a little pistou and serve at once.

THIS IS A REALLY DELICIOUS SOUP WHICH, WITH THE ADDITION OF PORCINI, CHICKEN AND PASTA, IS A MEAL IN ITSELF. YOU CAN BUY FRESH CHICKEN STOCK FROM MOST LARGE SUPERMARKETS OR, OF COURSE, MAKE YOUR OWN! HOWEVER, IF YOU DO USE PACKET STOCK, MAKE IT UP WEAKER THAN NORMAL AS IT CAN BE A LITTLE TOO SALTY.

Roasted tomato pesto pasta

SERVES 4

225G (8OZ) CHERRY TOMATOES

4 TABLESPOONS OLIVE OIL

1 LARGE SLICE WHITE BREAD, CUBED

450G (1LB) DRIED CONCHIGLIE, RIGATONI OR
   FUSILLI

1 CLOVE GARLIC, CRUSHED

1 CHILLI, DESEEDED AND CHOPPED

1 TABLESPOON SUN-DRIED TOMATO PASTE

SALT AND FRESHLY GROUND BLACK PEPPER

2 TABLESPOONS ROUGHLY TORN FRESH BASIL
   LEAVES

1. Preheat the oven to Gas Mark 6/200°C/400°F.

2. Place the cherry tomatoes in a roasting tin and
   drizzle with 1 tablespoon of the olive oil. Season
   and roast for 30 minutes.

3. Meanwhile, fry the bread cubes in 1 tablespoon of
   the oil, until golden and crisp. Set aside.

4. Cook the pasta in a pan of boiling water as
   directed on the packet and drain well when cooked.

5. Transfer the roasted tomatoes to a food processor,
   add the fried bread cubes, garlic, chilli, tomato
   paste and the remaining olive oil and season.
   Blend together and serve tossed through the pasta
   with the fresh basil.

Pasta ragout

SERVES 4

1 TABLESPOON OLIVE OIL

1 LEEK, SHREDDED

225G (8OZ) PORK FILLET, DICED

2 CARROTS, DICED

1 CLOVE GARLIC, CRUSHED

2 TEASPOONS PAPRIKA

¼ TEASPOON CAYENNE PEPPER

150ML (¼ PINT) WHITE WINE

600ML (1 PINT) VEGETABLE STOCK

1 x 400G (14OZ) CAN BORLOTTI BEANS,
    DRAINED AND RINSED

SALT AND FRESHLY GROUND BLACK PEPPER

175G (6OZ) QUICK-COOK DRIED VERMICELLI

175G (6OZ) SAVOY CABBAGE, SHREDDED

4 TABLESPOONS SOURED CREAM, TO SERVE

1. Heat the oil in a large frying pan or wok. Add the shredded leek and fry for 5 minutes. Stir in the pork and carrot and fry for a further 3-4 minutes until lightly browned. Add the garlic, paprika and cayenne pepper and fry for 1 minute.

2. Pour in the wine and 425ml (¾ pint) of the stock, add the drained borlotti beans and season well. Bring to the boil and simmer for 3 minutes.

3. Break up the vermicelli and stir into the pan. Sit the shredded cabbage on top of the pork and pasta ragout and cover with a lid. Simmer the ragout for a further 5 minutes, or until the pasta is cooked, adding more stock if the pan becomes too dry. Remove the lid and stir the cabbage through the ragout.

4. To serve, pile the ragout into individual serving dishes and drizzle over the soured cream.

Red onion & mustard pasta

SERVES 2-3

4 GOOD-QUALITY BUTCHER'S
    SAUSAGES

55-85G (2-3OZ) DRIED TAGLIATELLE
    PER PERSON

FOR THE SAUCE

25G (1OZ) UNSALTED BUTTER

150ML (¼ PINT) WHITE WINE

450G (1LB) RED ONIONS, CHOPPED

3 TABLESPOONS GRAINY MUSTARD

2 TABLESPOONS CHOPPED FRESH FLAT-LEAF
    PARSLEY

SALT AND FRESHLY GROUND BLACK PEPPER

1. To make the sauce, heat the butter and wine together in a large pan. Add the chopped red onion and cover with a tight-fitting lid. Sweat the onion over a low heat for 30 minutes until soft and transparent. Then remove the lid and increase the heat. Fry for a further 10-15 minutes, until a light golden colour.

2. Meanwhile, preheat the grill to a medium setting then grill the sausages for 12-15 minutes, turning frequently until cooked and golden.

3. While the sausages are cooking, cook the pasta in a pan of boiling water as directed on the packet.

4. Meanwhile, transfer the cooked onion to a small food processor or blender. Add the grainy mustard and blend until smooth. Stir in the chopped parsley and season.

5. To serve, drain the pasta well and toss with the onion sauce. Pile the dressed pasta on to 2 or 3 serving plates, grind over a little black pepper and serve at once with the grilled sausages.

4 speedy suppers

After a hard day's work, cooking up a meal can sometimes seem a real chore, and what's needed at the end of the day is a meal that is quick and easy to prepare yet filling and nourishing. The temptation to rely on ready-made pasta sauces may be great, but for the freshest, healthiest kick there are many speedy home-made options, too. With a trusty food processor to blitz your chosen ingredients, the choice of flavours becomes endless and opening a tub of pasta sauce will become a thing of the past. Alternatively, simply combine a handful of everyday ingredients with pasta and speedily transform them into impressive sumptuous dishes.

Once you have mastered the art of swift sauce making, all that is left for you to do is cook your favourite pasta, fresh or dried, and your nutritious mouthwatering meal is ready in no time. What could be easier?

Purple pesto

SERVES 4

450G (1LB) COOKED BEETROOT

55G (2OZ) FRESHLY GRATED PARMESAN
   CHEESE

1 BUNCH FRESH CHIVES, CHOPPED

1 CLOVE GARLIC, CRUSHED

SALT AND FRESHLY GROUND BLACK PEPPER

150ML (¼ PINT) OLIVE OIL

450G (1LB) DRIED OR FRESH PASTA SHELLS,
   TWISTS, SPIRALS OR BOWS

LEMON WEDGES, TO SERVE

1. Place the beetroot in a food processor and blend
   until chopped but not smooth. Add the Parmesan,
   chopped chives and garlic, season well and process
   again briefly. Stir in the olive oil and transfer to
   a saucepan.

2. Cook the pasta in a pan of boiling water as
   directed on the packet.

3. To serve, heat the pesto very gently. Drain the
   cooked pasta and toss with the pesto. Transfer to
   4 serving bowls and serve at once with wedges of
   lemon.

79

Red hot tomato sauce

MAKES ABOUT 400ML (14FL OZ)/ DRESSES ABOUT 350-450G (12OZ-1LB) UNCOOKED WEIGHT OF PASTA

1 x 400G (14OZ) CAN TOMATOES IN TOMATO JUICE

1 TABLESPOON SUN-DRIED TOMATO PASTE

1 TEASPOON CHILLI SAUCE, OR TO TASTE

SALT AND FRESHLY GROUND BLACK PEPPER

1. Place the canned tomatoes in a food processor and blend until smooth.

2. Transfer to a saucepan and add the remaining ingredients. Season to taste. Gently heat and use as required.

Black olive pesto

DRESSES ABOUT 450G (1LB) UNCOOKED WEIGHT OF PASTA

20 GREEK-STYLE BLACK OLIVES, PITTED

1 LARGE BEEFSTEAK TOMATO, SKINNED, SEEDED AND ROUGHLY CHOPPED

GRATED RIND OF 1 LEMON

1 CLOVE GARLIC, CRUSHED

25G (1OZ) FETA CHEESE, CRUMBLED

½ TABLESPOON CHOPPED FRESH YOUNG THYME LEAF

2 TABLESPOONS CHOPPED FRESH FLAT-LEAF PARSLEY

2 TABLESPOONS VIRGIN OLIVE OIL

FRESHLY GROUND BLACK PEPPER

1. Place all the ingredients in a food processor with 1 tablespoon of the flat-leaf parsley and process together. Season with black pepper and serve tossed through your favourite pasta with the remaining chopped parsley. Serve at once.

Hey pesto

DRESSES ABOUT 450G (1LB)
UNCOOKED WEIGHT OF PASTA

40G (1½OZ) FRESH BASIL LEAVES

25G (1OZ) FLAT-LEAF PARSLEY

55G (2OZ) PARMESAN CHEESE, GRATED

2 CLOVES GARLIC, CRUSHED

85-125ML (3-4FL OZ) VIRGIN OLIVE OIL

SALT AND FRESHLY GROUND BLACK PEPPER

1. Place all the ingredients in a food processor and process together with enough oil to make a well-blended paste. Season to taste and serve at once tossed through freshly cooked pasta.

Broccoli spears with lemon & parmesan

SERVES 2

225G (8OZ) DRIED RIGATONI

350G (12OZ) BROCCOLI SPEARS

2 TABLESPOONS VIRGIN OLIVE OIL

1 CLOVE GARLIC, CRUSHED

JUICE OF ½ LEMON

SALT AND FRESHLY GROUND BLACK PEPPER

LEMON WEDGES, TO SERVE

FRESHLY GRATED PARMESAN CHEESE, TO SERVE

1. Cook the pasta in a large pan of boiling water as directed on the packet. Add the broccoli spears for the last 2-3 minutes of cooking time.

2. Meanwhile, mix the oil, garlic and lemon juice together in a small bowl.

3. Drain the cooked pasta and broccoli and toss with the oil, garlic and lemon juice. Season well and serve at once with lemon wedges. Hand around the Parmesan cheese separately.

BROCCOLI, AN EXCELLENT SOURCE OF VITAMIN C AND RICH IN VITAMIN A, COMES TO LIFE IN THIS SIMPLE BUT MOUTHWATERING PASTA DISH.

Minted pasta with lettuce & peas

SERVES 2

25G (1OZ) BUTTER

1 LARGE ONION, FINELY CHOPPED

150ML (¼ PINT) WHITE WINE

225G (8OZ) FROZEN PETIT POIS

SALT AND FRESHLY GROUND BLACK PEPPER

225G (8OZ) FRESH RICCIOLI

40G (1½OZ) ROUND LETTUCE, SHREDDED

2 TABLESPOONS CHOPPED FRESH MINT

2 TABLESPOONS CRÈME FRAÎCHE

1. Heat the butter in a large pan. Add the chopped onion and fry for 5 minutes until softened. Pour in the wine and cook for 1 minute. Add the frozen peas and season. Simmer for 4-5 minutes, until the peas are just cooked.

2. Meanwhile, cook the pasta in a pan of boiling water as directed on the packet.

3. To serve, add the shredded lettuce and chopped mint to the peas. Drain the pasta and toss with the minted peas. Transfer into serving bowls. Top each with a blob of crème fraîche and serve at once.

DON'T THINK OF LETTUCE JUST FOR THE SALAD PLATE. LIGHTLY COOKED, IT MAKES A GREAT PARTNER TO PEAS AND MINT, AND A SUBSTANTIAL MEAL WHEN TOSSED, AS HERE, WITH PASTA AND CRÈME FRAÎCHE.

Dolcelatte, rocket & walnut linguini

SERVES 2

175G (6OZ) FRESH LINGUINI OR PENNE

115G (4OZ) ROCKET LEAVES

115G (4OZ) DOLCELATTE CHEESE

1 TABLESPOON WALNUT OIL

SALT AND FRESHLY GROUND BLACK PEPPER

1. Cook the pasta in a pan of boiling water as directed on the packet.

2. Place the rocket in a large serving bowl. Using your fingers, break the cheese into small pieces and add to the rocket. Pour over the walnut oil and season well.

3. To serve, drain the pasta and toss it in the rocket and dolcelatte mixture. Serve at once.

THIS IS ONE OF MY FAVOURITE PASTA DISHES. AS THE FRESHLY COOKED PASTA IS TOSSED THROUGH, THE CHEESE MELTS AND THE ROCKET WILTS. REALLY FABULOUS!

Spaghetti with garlic & herb spring greens

SERVES 4

8 RASHERS STREAKY BACON

350G (12OZ) DRIED SPAGHETTI

1 TABLESPOON OLIVE OIL

450G (1LB) SPRING GREENS, SHREDDED AND
    WASHED

1 X 150G (5OZ) GARLIC AND HERB SOFT WHITE
    CHEESE, ROUGHLY MASHED WITH A FORK

SALT AND FRESHLY GROUND BLACK PEPPER

1. Preheat the grill to a medium setting. Place the bacon under the grill and cook until crisp. Set aside to cool.

2. Cook the spaghetti in a pan of boiling water as directed on the packet.

3. Meanwhile, heat the oil in a large frying pan or wok. Add the spring greens and stir-fry for 1 minute. Cover, reduce the heat slightly and cook for a further 5 minutes.

4. Crumble the grilled bacon into small pieces.

5. To serve, drain the spaghetti and add immediately to the cooked greens. Add the mashed garlic and herb cheese, season and toss together well. Transfer to a serving dish, scatter with the crispy bacon bits and serve at once.

THIS IS A FABULOUS WAY OF EATING AND ENJOYING YOUR GREENS. BE GENEROUS WITH THE BLACK PEPPER.

Fiery pepper pâté

DRESSES ABOUT 175-225G
(6-8OZ) UNCOOKED WEIGHT
OF PASTA

25G (1OZ) SUN-DRIED PEPPER

100ML (3½FL OZ) BOILING WATER

1 TABLESPOON FRESHLY GRATED PARMESAN
    CHEESE

1 RED CHILLI, DESEEDED AND CHOPPED

1 TABLESPOON TOASTED PINE NUTS

3 TABLESPOONS OLIVE OIL

SALT AND FRESHLY GROUND BLACK PEPPER

1. Soak the sun-dried pepper in the boiling water and set aside for 30 minutes.

2. Transfer the soaked pepper with all of its soaking liquid to a small food processor or pestle and mortar. Add all the remaining ingredients and blend or pound together to form a pâté, adding a little hot water if needed. Season to taste, and serve stirred through freshly cooked pasta.

STIR THIS CREAMY AND LUSH PÂTÉ THROUGH FRESHLY COOKED PASTA OR SIMPLY SPREAD IT ON THICK SLICES OF TOASTED BREAD.

5 something special

You may have ignored pasta as an option for that special occasion, but now is the time to put it back on the menu. This chapter comprises recipes that are ideal for entertaining or for any family celebration. They are simply a bit 'different': some include alcohol, such as white wine, vermouth and brandy; others team pasta with unusual combinations of ingredients. Present your guests with individual parcels of spaghetti or tagliatelle with dolcelatte cheese and roasted fennel, and they will never look at pasta in the same way again. Whatever your preferences for pasta and noodles, there is bound to be something here to capture your imagination and tantalize your tastebuds.

Crispy duck with gingered noodles

SERVES 4-6

1 WHOLE DUCK, ABOUT 1.5KG (3LB)

1 TEASPOON SALT

225G (8OZ) MEDIUM EGG NOODLES

1 TABLESPOON VEGETABLE OIL

1 BUNCH SPRING ONIONS, CHOPPED

2 LARGE CARROTS, PEELED AND CUT INTO VERY
    FINE STRIPS

225G (8OZ) BEAN SPROUTS

225G (8OZ) RED SWISS CHARD, ROUGHLY
    SHREDDED

1 CLOVE GARLIC, CRUSHED

2.5CM (1 INCH) PIECE OF FRESH ROOT GINGER,
    PEELED AND FINELY CHOPPED

2 TABLESPOONS SOY SAUCE

JUICE OF 1 ORANGE

JUICE OF 1 LIME

1 BUNCH FRESH CORIANDER, ROUGHLY CHOPPED

1. Preheat the oven to Gas Mark 6/200°C/400°F.

2. Using a fork, prick the duck all over and lightly rub over the salt. Place the duck on a rack set over a roasting tin and place in the oven for about 1¼ hours, until crisp and cooked.

3. Cook the noodles in a pan of boiling water as directed on the packet. Drain well and set aside.

4. Remove the duck from the oven and set aside to cool slightly. Then, using a sharp knife and fork, pull and chop the meat and skin from the carcass and spread out on a baking tray. Return the shredded duck to the oven for 5 minutes.

5. Meanwhile, heat the oil in a large wok. Add the spring onions, carrots, bean sprouts and Swiss chard and stir-fry for 2 minutes. Add the garlic, ginger, soy sauce, orange and lime juice, then toss in the noodles and season.

6. To serve, pile the dressed noodles into 4 dishes and top with the crispy duck. Scatter over the chopped coriander and serve at once.

ROASTING THE DUCK ON A RACK WITH SALT WILL ENSURE THAT THE SKIN GOES CRISPY. YOU CAN MAKE THIS TASTY DISH USING EITHER A WHOLE DUCK OR DUCK LEGS. YOU WILL NEED AT LEAST 4 LEGS AND THE ROASTING TIME WILL BE A LITTLE LESS - ABOUT 40 MINUTES.

Roasted pumpkin chutney with fusilli

SERVES 4

1 x 1.8KG (4LB) PUMPKIN, PEELED, DESEEDED
   AND CUT INTO 2.5CM (1 INCH) CHUNKS

1 SPRIG OF ROSEMARY

2 TABLESPOONS BROWN SUGAR

2 TABLESPOONS BALSAMIC VINEGAR

3 TABLESPOONS OLIVE OIL

SALT AND FRESHLY GROUND BLACK PEPPER

280G (10OZ) FRESH FUSILLI

140G (5OZ) MILD CREAMY GOAT'S CHEESE

4 TABLESPOONS FRESH BASIL LEAVES

1. Preheat the oven to Gas Mark 6/200°C/400°F.

2. Place the pumpkin chunks and the rosemary in a roasting tin and sprinkle over the brown sugar, balsamic vinegar and olive oil. Season well and roast for 40 minutes, turning frequently.

3. Ten minutes before the pumpkin is cooked, cook the pasta spirals in a pan of boiling water as directed on the packet.

4. To serve, drain the pasta, return it to the pan it was cooked in and toss in the roasted pumpkin with all of its juices. Crumble in the goat's cheese and gently stir through the basil leaves. Serve at once

THERE'S PLENTY OF PUMPKIN ABOUT IN THE AUTUMN. IT'S INEXPENSIVE AND TASTY AND A GREAT PARTNER FOR PASTA, ESPECIALLY WHEN ROASTED.

Houmous pepper pasta

SERVES 2

2 RED PEPPERS

1½ TABLESPOONS OLIVE OIL

175G (6OZ) DRIED VERMICELLI

SQUEEZE OF LEMON JUICE

SALT AND FRESHLY GROUND BLACK PEPPER

LARGE HANDFUL ROCKET LEAVES

FOR THE HOUMOUS
DRESSING

5 TABLESPOONS HOUMOUS

3 TABLESPOONS GREEK YOGURT

JUICE OF ½ LEMON

1. Preheat the oven to Gas Mark 6/200°C/400°F.

2. Rub the whole peppers with a little of the olive oil and place on a baking tray. Bake in the oven for 40-45 minutes, until cooked and lightly charred.

3. Towards the end of the cooking time, cook the vermicelli in a pan of boiling water as directed on the packet.

4. To make the houmous dressing, combine the houmous, Greek yogurt and lemon juice in a small bowl. Season well and set aside.

5. To serve, drain the vermicelli well and toss with the remaining oil and a squeeze of lemon juice, then season. Pile the pasta into 2 serving bowls and drizzle over the houmous dressing. Top each with some rocket leaves and a whole roasted pepper. Serve at once.

Spaghetti & mussels baked in a bag

SERVES 4

250G (9OZ) DRIED SPAGHETTI

1 X 400G (14OZ) CAN CHERRY TOMATOES

2 TABLESPOONS SUN-DRIED TOMATO PASTE

2 CLOVES GARLIC, CRUSHED

12 GREEK-STYLE BLACK OLIVES, PITTED AND
     ROUGHLY CHOPPED

1 BUNCH FRESH PARSLEY, ROUGHLY CHOPPED

SALT AND FRESHLY GROUND BLACK PEPPER

24 SMALL LIVE MUSSELS, CLEANED

FRESHLY GRATED PARMESAN CHEESE, TO SERVE

HOT CRUSTY BREAD, TO SERVE

1. Preheat the oven to Gas Mark 5/190°C/375°F.

2. Cook the spaghetti in a pan of boiling water as directed on the packet until just cooked.

3. Meanwhile, combine the canned tomatoes, sun-dried tomato paste, crushed garlic, black olives and parsley in a bowl. Season well.

4. Cut out 4 pieces of foil and 4 pieces of greaseproof paper, all approximately 38 x 30cm (15 x 12 inches). Lay the pieces of greaseproof paper on a working surface and overlay each with a piece of foil.

5. Drain the pasta and toss with the tomato and olive sauce. Divide the dressed pasta into 4, placing a mound on each piece of foil. Top each mound with 6 mussels and bring together the corners of each piece to close each parcel, trapping a little air in each. Seal the edges well by twisting them together.

6. Transfer the parcels to baking trays and place in the oven for 20-25 minutes to allow the mussels to cook and open.

7. To serve, place the parcels on individual serving plates, and serve with the freshly grated Parmesan, accompanied by hot crusty bread.

HERE IS YET ANOTHER EASY WAY OF COOKING MUSSELS. ALLOW YOUR GUESTS TO OPEN THEIR OWN BAGS AND SPRINKLE WITH A GENEROUS SPOONFUL OF GRATED PARMESAN.

Sausage & cranberry pasta bake

SERVES 4

450G (1LB) GOOD-QUALITY BUTCHER'S
   SAUSAGES
½ TABLESPOON OLIVE OIL
25G (1OZ) BUTTER
1 ONION, SLICED
2 TABLESPOONS FLOUR
425ML (¾ PINT) CHICKEN STOCK
150ML (¼ PINT) PORT
1 x 70G (2½OZ) PACKET DRIED CRANBERRIES
LARGE SPRIG OF THYME
1 BAY LEAF
SALT AND FRESHLY GROUND BLACK PEPPER
225G (8OZ) FRESH PENNE
85G (3OZ) GRUYÈRE CHEESE, GRATED

1. Preheat the oven to Gas Mark 7/220°C/425°F.

2. Divide each sausage into 2, by twisting and then snipping the skin. Toss them with the oil in a large shallow ovenproof dish. Roast in the oven for 30-35 minutes, until browned.

3. Meanwhile, heat the butter in a frying pan. Add the sliced onion and fry for 5 minutes until golden. Stir in the flour and cook for 1 minute. Remove from the heat and stir in the chicken stock and port. Return to the heat and bring to the boil, stirring. Add the dried cranberries, the thyme and bay leaf, and season. Simmer for 5 minutes.

4. Cook the pasta in a pan of boiling water as directed on the packet. Drain well.

5. When the sausages are browned, remove them from the oven and reduce the oven temperature to Gas Mark 6/200°C/400°F. Drain off any excess fat and add the cooked pasta to the dish. Pour over the cranberry sauce and mix together. Scatter with the grated Gruyère and return to the oven for 15-20 minutes, until bubbling and golden. Serve at once.

CRANBERRIES HAVE A DISTINCT TART FLAVOUR AND WORK WELL WITH RICH, MEATY SAUSAGES AND CHEESY PASTA.

Pappardelle pork with armagnac sauce

SERVES 4

450G (1LB) PORK FILLET, CUT INTO 4 EQUAL
    PIECES

4 LARGE FRESH SAGE LEAVES, ROUGHLY
    CHOPPED

SALT AND FRESHLY GROUND BLACK PEPPER

4 SLICES PARMA HAM

1 TABLESPOON OLIVE OIL

6 TABLESPOONS ARMAGNAC OR OTHER BRANDY

300ML (½ PINT) CHICKEN STOCK

200ML (7FL OZ) DOUBLE CREAM

225G (8OZ) DRIED PAPPARDELLE

15G (½OZ) BUTTER

2 TABLESPOONS CHOPPED FRESH FLAT-LEAF
    PARSLEY

1. Preheat the oven to Gas Mark 6/200°C/400°F.

2. Using a sharp knife, cut a horizontal slice, three-quarters of the way through each piece of pork fillet. Stuff each slit with a sage leaf. Season well and wrap each fillet in a piece of Parma ham.

3. Heat the olive oil in a large pan. Add the wrapped pork fillet pieces and cook for 1-2 minutes, turning once, until the Parma ham is golden brown. Transfer to a baking tray and bake in the oven for 10-12 minutes, or until the pork is cooked.

4. Meanwhile, return the frying pan to the heat and add the brandy. Using a wooden spoon, stir vigorously, scraping the bottom of the pan. Boil for 1 minute. Add the chicken stock and boil for a further 2 minutes. Add the cream and boil again for 2-3 minutes, until the sauce has thickened slightly. Season to taste.

5. Cook the pasta in a pan of boiling water as directed on the packet.

6. Remove the pork from the oven and pour any cooking juices from the baking tray into the armagnac sauce. Cover the pork with foil and leave to rest for 5 minutes.

7. To serve, drain the pappardelle and stir in the butter and parsley. Season well. Divide between 4 serving plates and spoon over the brandy sauce. Cut each piece of pork fillet into 4 slices and place on the top of the pasta servings. Serve at once.

THE FRESH TANG OF THE SAGE IS A MUST IN THIS
DECADENT MEATY DISH.

Roasted vegetables in wine with basil fettuccine

SERVES 4

55G (2OZ) BUTTER

150ML (¼ PINT) WHITE WINE

3 PARSNIPS, PEELED AND DICED

1 CELERIAC, PEELED AND DICED

1 LARGE ONION, CHOPPED

3 LARGE CARROTS, PEELED AND DICED

1 BAY LEAF

200G (7OZ) CHERRY TOMATOES, HALVED

225–280G (8–10OZ) FRESH FETTUCCINE

1 TABLESPOON OLIVE OIL

4 TABLESPOONS SOURED CREAM

1 BUNCH FRESH BASIL LEAVES, ROUGHLY TORN

SEA SALT AND FRESHLY GROUND BLACK PEPPER

1. Preheat the oven to Gas Mark 6/200°C/400°F.

2. Place the butter and wine in a large roasting tin and place in the oven for 5 minutes until the butter is melted. Remove from the oven and add the parsnips, celeriac, onion, carrots and bay leaf. Return to the oven for 1–1¼ hours, until the vegetables are cooked and slightly browned. Five minutes before the end of the cooking time stir in the cherry tomatoes.

3. Meanwhile, cook the fettuccine in a pan of boiling water as directed on the packet and drain.

4. To serve, toss the warm fettuccine in the olive oil and divide between 4 serving dishes. Top each with a drizzle of soured cream and then a mound of the roasted vegetables. Scatter with torn basil leaves and finish with a sprinkling of sea salt and freshly ground black pepper.

SWEET, RICH ROOT VEGETABLES REIGN IN THIS RECIPE WITH AMAZING RESULTS.

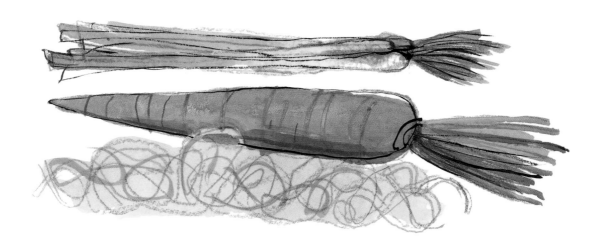

Spaghetti with vermouth mussels

SERVES 4

900G (2LB) MUSSELS

55G (2OZ) BUTTER

150ML (¼ PINT) DRY VERMOUTH

1 CLOVE GARLIC, CRUSHED

1 BUNCH FRESH FLAT-LEAF PARSLEY, CHOPPED

350G (12OZ) FRESH SPAGHETTI

150ML (¼ PINT) DOUBLE CREAM

FRESHLY GROUND BLACK PEPPER

1. Clean the mussels by scrubbing them and soaking well in cold water. Pull away all the seaweed threads. Discard any mussels that are cracked or remain open when tapped.

2. Heat the butter in a large saucepan. Add the vermouth, garlic and half of the parsley. Simmer for 1 minute. Add the mussels, cover the pan tightly with a lid and leave to steam over a medium heat for 3-5 minutes, or until the mussels have opened.

3. Meanwhile, cook the spaghetti in a pan of boiling water as directed on the packet.

4. Remove the mussels from the cooking liquid and keep warm, discarding any mussels that have not opened. Add the cream to the liquid in the pan and bring to the boil. Season with black pepper and simmer for 1 minute.

5. To serve, drain the spaghetti and transfer to 4 serving bowls. Top each with some mussels and spoon over the vermouth and cream sauce. Scatter with the remaining parsley and serve at once.

MOULES MARINIÈRE, VERMOUTH-STYLE - SERVE THEM STEAMING HOT OVER A BED OF SPAGHETTI WITH PLENTY OF CRUSTY GARLIC BREAD.

Pasta blanc with tarragon chicken

SERVES 4

1 TABLESPOON OIL

8 RASHERS SMOKED STREAKY BACON, CUT IN
    HALF WIDTHWAYS

3 LARGE CHICKEN BREASTS, CUT INTO CHUNKY
    STRIPS

2 HEAPED TABLESPOONS GRAINY MUSTARD

150ML (¼ PINT) WHITE WINE

2 TABLESPOONS CHOPPED FRESH TARRAGON

200ML (7FL OZ) DOUBLE CREAM

SALT AND FRESHLY GROUND BLACK PEPPER

280G (10OZ) LARGE PASTA SHELLS

LEMON WEDGES, TO SERVE

1. Heat the oil in a large pan. Add the bacon and fry for 5 minutes. Toss the chicken in the mustard in a bowl then add to the pan. Fry for 4-5 minutes.

2. Add the white wine and chopped tarragon to the pan and bring to the boil. Simmer for 5 minutes, or until the chicken is just cooked. Stir in the double cream, season, and simmer for 5 minutes.

3. Meanwhile, cook the pasta shells in a pan of boiling water as directed on the packet.

4. To serve, drain the pasta and toss with the mustard and tarragon chicken. Serve at once, accompanied by the lemon wedges.

Fennel chips with dolcelatte pasta

SERVES 4

2 HEADS FENNEL, WITH THE TOPS RESERVED

2 TABLESPOONS OLIVE OIL

SALT AND FRESHLY GROUND BLACK PEPPER

300ML (½ PINT) WHITE WINE

225G (8OZ) DOLCELATTE CHEESE, CRUMBLED

350G (12OZ) SPINACH AND PLAIN DRIED
    TAGLIATELLE

1. Preheat the oven to Gas Mark 6/200°C/400°F.

2. Cut each fennel bulb into 8 wedges, place in a roasting tin and toss with the olive oil. Season well. Place in the oven and roast for 1-1¼ hours, until the fennel is softened and lightly charred.

3. When the fennel is almost ready, pour the wine into a saucepan and simmer until reduced by about half. Stir in the crumbled dolcelatte and heat gently until melted.

4. Meanwhile, cook the pasta in a pan of boiling water as directed on the packet.

5. To serve, drain the pasta and toss with the wine and cheese sauce. Season with black pepper and scatter over the reserved fennel tops. Serve at once, topped with the roasted fennel.

Game sausages with parsnip penne

SERVES 4

6 VENISON OR GAME SAUSAGES

225G (8OZ) FRESH PENNE

85G (3OZ) BUTTER

1 TABLESPOON RUNNY HONEY

450G (1LB) PARSNIPS, PEELED AND GRATED

JUICE OF 1 ORANGE

2 TABLESPOONS CHOPPED FRESH FLAT-LEAF
    PARSLEY

2 TABLESPOONS CHOPPED FRESH CHIVES

SALT AND FRESHLY GROUND BLACK PEPPER

1. Preheat the grill to a medium setting.

2. Grill the sausages for 12-15 minutes, turning them frequently until golden and cooked.

3. Meanwhile, cook the pasta in a pan of boiling water as directed on the packet.

4. Melt 55g (2oz) of the butter in a large frying pan or wok. Add the honey and mix well, then add the grated parsnips. Stir-fry for 5-6 minutes, or until the parsnips are tender and beginning to colour. Season well, stir in the orange juice and cook for 2 minutes. Stir in the fresh herbs.

5. To serve, drain the pasta and toss with the remaining butter. Season with black pepper and divide between 4 serving plates. Top each with some parsnip hash then cut each sausage in half diagonally and place three halves on the top of each dish. Serve at once.

THIS SWEET PARSNIP HASH IS MOUTHWATERINGLY GOOD WITH GAMEY SAUSAGES, OR ANY GOOD-QUALITY PORK SAUSAGE FOR THAT MATTER.

Coconut & chilli noodles

SERVES 4

225G (8OZ) RICE NOODLES

1 TABLESPOON GRAPESEED OR VEGETABLE OIL

1 CLOVE GARLIC, PEELED

450G (1LB) RAW TIGER PRAWNS, PEELED WITH
    THE TAILS LEFT ON

JUICE OF ½ LIME

1 BUNCH FRESH CORIANDER, ROUGHLY CHOPPED

FOR THE SAUCE

2 GREEN CHILLIES, DESEEDED AND CHOPPED

2.5CM (1 INCH) PIECE OF FRESH ROOT GINGER,
    PEELED AND ROUGHLY CHOPPED

175G (6OZ) CASHEW NUTS, TOASTED

JUICE OF ½ LIME

1 CLOVE GARLIC, CRUSHED

200ML (7FL OZ) COCONUT CREAM

150ML (¼ PINT) WARM WATER

SALT AND FRESHLY GROUND BLACK PEPPER

1. To make the sauce, blend together the chillies, ginger, cashew nuts, lime juice, garlic, coconut cream and warm water in a food processor. Season and transfer the mixture to a saucepan.

2. Cook the rice noodles in a pan of boiling water as directed on the packet. Place the coconut and chilli sauce over a very low heat to warm gently. Stir occasionally and add a little extra water if the sauce is too thick.

3. Meanwhile, heat the oil in a large frying pan and add the whole peeled garlic clove. Fry for 30 seconds, then remove and discard. Add the prawns to the pan and stir-fry for 3-4 minutes until they are pink and cooked. Sprinkle over the lime juice.

4. To serve, drain the noodles well and toss with the chopped coriander. Pile into 4 warm serving bowls and spoon over the coconut and chilli sauce. Top the sauce with the tiger prawns and serve at once.

Seared tuna with pasta & horseradish salad

SERVES 2

2 TUNA STEAKS

1½ TABLESPOONS OLIVE OIL

SQUEEZE OF LEMON JUICE

FRESHLY GROUND BLACK PEPPER

175G (6OZ) DRIED SPINACH TAGLIATELLE

LARGE HANDFUL BABY SPINACH LEAVES,
    COARSELY SHREDDED

FOR THE HORSERADISH
SALAD

1 TABLESPOON OLIVE OIL

350G (12OZ) ONIONS, CHOPPED

3 TABLESPOONS MAYONNAISE

5 TEASPOONS CREAMED HORSERADISH

1. Lay the tuna steaks in a shallow dish and pour over 1 tablespoon of the olive oil and a squeeze of lemon juice. Season with black pepper and set aside.

2. To make the salad, heat the oil in a large pan. Add the chopped onions and cover the pan with a disc of damp greaseproof paper and a tight-fitting lid. Sweat the onions over a very low heat for 30-45 minutes, until very soft and transparent.

3. Transfer the onions to a food processor and blend until smooth. Set aside to cool, then combine with the mayonnaise and horseradish and season to taste.

4. Cook the pasta as directed on the packet, then drain and toss in the remaining olive oil.

5. Heat a griddle pan and sear the tuna steaks for 2-3 minutes on each side or until just cooked.

6. To serve, pile the tagliatelle into 2 serving bowls and spoon over some horseradish salad. Top with the spinach leaves and a seared tuna steak. Serve at once.

6 Designer Dishes

Sexy, sassy and stylish, these designer dishes are perfect for a special dinner, a luscious lunch or simply when you wish to indulge. Cheats' caviar is partnered by grilled smoked salmon, linguini is dressed in roasted asparagus and pancetta and a hot juniper vinaigrette laces a delicious dish of smoked trout and papardelle with a hint of gin. Using luxury ingredients need not mean that these recipes are complicated or time-consuming to prepare - they are simply a little more sumptuous in their approach than usual and involve impressive presentation of some exotic ingredients. All the recipes in this section are certain to make an impact and with the minimum of preparation you can create a truly elegant meal.

Smoked trout with juniper vinaigrette

SERVES 2-3

150ML (¼ PINT) WHITE WINE

1 TABLESPOON WHITE WINE VINEGAR

1 BAY LEAF

6 JUNIPER BERRIES, CRUSHED

175G (6OZ) DRIED PAPPARDELLE

3 TABLESPOONS OLIVE OIL

SALT AND FRESHLY GROUND BLACK PEPPER

1 BUNCH FRESH DILL, CHOPPED

225G (8OZ) SMOKED TROUT, ROUGHLY
  BROKEN UP

2 LARGE CARROTS, PEELED AND CUT INTO
  RIBBONS

1. Heat together the wine, wine vinegar, bay leaf and crushed juniper berries in a pan. Bring to the boil and simmer until reduced by half.

2. Meanwhile, cook the pasta in a pan of boiling water as directed on the packet.

3. When the juniper dressing is reduced, remove it from the heat, whisk in the oil and season to taste.

4. Drain the cooked pasta and toss with the juniper dressing, most of the chopped dill, the smoked trout and carrot ribbons. Serve warm or cold, scattered with a little more dill.

JUNIPER IS MOST FAMILIAR AS THE FLAVOURING USED IN GIN. THESE PUNGENT BERRIES ARE GREAT IN GAME STEWS, BUT ARE USED HERE WITH RICH SMOKED TROUT. THEY ARE EASILY CRUSHED USING THE BACK OF A SPOON.

Egg lasagne with wild mushroom fricassée

SERVES 4

55G (2OZ) CREAM CHEESE

125ML (4FL OZ) CRÈME FRAÎCHE

4 TABLESPOONS CHOPPED FRESH PARSLEY

SALT AND FRESHLY GROUND BLACK PEPPER

55G (2OZ) UNSALTED BUTTER

1 ONION, CHOPPED

175G (6OZ) LARGE FIELD MUSHROOMS, SLICED

280G (10OZ) MIXED MUSHROOMS (SHIITAKE, OYSTER, BUTTON), CUT INTO BITE-SIZED PIECES

1 CLOVE GARLIC, CRUSHED

1 TABLESPOON BALSAMIC VINEGAR

8 LARGE SHEETS FRESH EGG LASAGNE

1. Combine the cream cheese, crème fraîche and half of the parsley in a bowl. Season well and set aside.

2. Heat the unsalted butter in a large pan. Add the chopped onion and fry gently for 8-10 minutes until softened. Increase the heat and add all of the mushrooms and the garlic. Fry for 4-5 minutes until the mushrooms are cooked. Add the balsamic vinegar and the remaining chopped parsley to the hot pan and season.

3. Meanwhile, soak the lasagne as directed on the packet then cook it in a pan of boiling water, as directed, and drain well.

4. For each serving, lay a sheet of lasagne on a serving plate and spread with a quarter of the cream cheese mixture. Top each with a quarter of the hot mushrooms and cover with another sheet of lasagne to form a sandwich, folding it back slightly to reveal the filling. Serve at once.

Crispy sardines on linguini with lemon beurre blanc

SERVES 4-6

12 LARGE SARDINES

350G (12OZ) FRESH LINGUINI

4 TABLESPOONS MANGO AND LIME CHUTNEY

1 BUNCH FRESH FLAT-LEAF PARSLEY, CHOPPED

LEMON WEDGES, TO SERVE

FOR THE SAUCE

40G (1½OZ) UNSALTED BUTTER

1 SHALLOT, FINELY CHOPPED

150ML (¼ PINT) WHITE WINE

300ML (½ PINT) DOUBLE CREAM

JUICE OF ½ LEMON

FRESHLY GROUND BLACK PEPPER

1. To prepare the sardines, remove the heads and make a cut along the belly from the head end to the tail. Clean out the fish under cold running water to remove the innards. Place each fish, cut side down on a board and lightly push down along the back bone to loosen it. Turn the flattened fish over, take the head end of the backbone and gently ease it and its attached bones up and away from the fish. Fold each fish back over to reform a fish shape, lightly slash each side and set aside.

2. Preheat the grill to its highest setting.

3. To make the sauce, heat 15g (½oz) of the butter in a saucepan and gently fry the shallot for 5 minutes. Add the wine and reduce by half. Stir in the cream and simmer for 5 minutes. Stir in the remaining butter and the lemon juice and season with black pepper.

4. Meanwhile, cook the pasta in a pan of boiling water as directed on the packet.

5. Spread the sardines with the mango and lime chutney and place them under the hot grill for 2-3 minutes each side, until golden and cooked.

6. Drain the pasta, toss with the hot lemon sauce and arrange on a long serving plate. Line the cooked sardines on top of the pasta and scatter with the flat-leaf parsley. Serve at once, garnished with lemon wedges.

HERE, FRESH SARDINES, CRISPED UP UNDER THE GRILL WITH A HINT OF MANGO AND LIME, ARE SERVED ON A BED OF PIPING HOT LINGUINI WITH LEMON SAUCE.

Wrapped salmon scallops with tagliatelle

SERVES 2

175G (6OZ) FRESH SPINACH TAGLIATELLE

1 TABLESPOON OLIVE OIL

2 x 115G (4OZ) SKINLESS BONELESS SALMON
FILLETS

4 TABLESPOONS WHITE WINE

2 HEAPED TABLESPOONS CRÈME FRAÎCHE

15G (½OZ) BUTTER

1 BUNCH FRESH CHIVES, CHOPPED

SALT AND FRESHLY GROUND BLACK PEPPER

1. Preheat the oven to Gas Mark 6/200°C/400°F.

2. Cook the tagliatelle in a pan of boiling water, as directed on the packet. Drain and transfer to a large bowl. Toss with the olive oil and set aside.

3. Take each salmon fillet and using a sharp knife, slice down the length, on a slant, cutting each one into about 5mm (¼ inch) slices. Keeping the slices together, push down gently with the palm of your hand to fan them out slightly.

4. Take two large pieces of thick tin foil and mound the cooked tagliatelle into the centre of each. Top each mound with a fillet of salmon scallops. Combine the white wine and crème fraîche in a bowl and spoon over the salmon and pasta. Finish each with a knob of butter and a generous scattering of chopped chives. Season well.

5. Bring up the sides of the foil to form loose parcels and transfer to a baking tray.

6. Bake for 15-20 minutes, until the salmon is cooked. To serve, place each parcel on a large dinner plate and take straight to the table.

HERE, SALMON IS STEAMED IN AN AROMATIC PARCEL WITH TAGLIATELLE, WINE AND CHIVES. ALLOW YOUR GUESTS TO OPEN THEIR PARCELS AT THE TABLE AND INHALE THE LOVELY AROMA. SLICING THE SALMON IN THIS WAY HELPS REDUCE THE COOKING TIME AND MAKES IT EASY TO EAT.

Fusilli gingered crab

SERVES 4

280g (10oz) DRIED SPINACH FUSILLI

175g (6oz) BROCCOLI FLORETS

4cm (1½ INCH) PIECE OF FRESH ROOT GINGER,
PEELED AND ROUGHLY CHOPPED

GRATED RIND OF 1 ORANGE

JUICE OF 2 ORANGES

1 BUNCH SPRING ONIONS, ROUGHLY CHOPPED

2 TABLESPOONS MEDIUM SHERRY

1 TABLESPOON DARK SOY SAUCE

150ML (¼ PINT) DOUBLE CREAM

SALT AND FRESHLY GROUND BLACK PEPPER

225g (8oz) FRESH WHITE CRAB MEAT

1. Cook the fusilli in a pan of boiling water as directed on the packet, adding the broccoli florets to the pan for the last 3 minutes of cooking.

2. Meanwhile, blend the ginger, orange rind and juice and spring onions together in a food processor. Transfer to a saucepan and stir in the sherry and soy sauce. Bring to the boil and simmer for 5 minutes. Stir in the double cream, season well and simmer for a further 1 minute.

3. To serve, drain the pasta and broccoli and gently toss with the crab meat. Divide between 4 serving bowls and spoon over the orange and ginger sauce. Serve at once.

THIS CRAB AND BROCCOLI PASTA IS SERVED WITH A WONDERFUL GINGER AND ORANGE SAUCE. FRESH ROOT GINGER IS NOW WIDELY AVAILABLE AND WILL KEEP FOR SEVERAL WEEKS, WRAPPED, IN THE REFRIGERATOR. WHEN BUYING GINGER ROOT, CHOOSE A PIECE THAT LOOKS AS SMOOTH AND FAT AS POSSIBLE. REMOVE THE SKIN WITH A SMALL KNIFE OR POTATO PEELER, AND GRATE OR CHOP IT VERY FINELY.

Hot pot penne with lamb and pepper jam

SERVES 4

4 x 115G (4OZ) LAMB CHUMP CHOPS

3 TABLESPOONS OLIVE OIL

1 TABLESPOON CRACKED BLACK PEPPER

2 ORANGE PEPPERS, SLICED

2 YELLOW PEPPERS, SLICED

1 RED PEPPER, SLICED

1 CLOVE GARLIC, CRUSHED

1 BAY LEAF

1 SPRIG OF ROSEMARY

1 TABLESPOON WINE VINEGAR

PINCH OF SUGAR

SALT AND FRESHLY GROUND BLACK PEPPER

150ML (¼ PINT) WHITE WINE

425ML (¾ PINT) VEGETABLE STOCK

225G (8OZ) FRESH PENNE

1. Place the lamb chops in a shallow dish. Spoon over 2 tablespoons of the olive oil and the cracked black pepper and set aside.

2. Heat the remaining oil in a large flameproof shallow pan or casserole dish. Add the peppers, garlic, bay leaf, rosemary, wine vinegar and sugar. Season well. Cover and cook over a low heat for 40-45 minutes, until the peppers are very soft.

3. Preheat the oven to Gas Mark 6/200°C/400°F.

4. Add the white wine and vegetable stock to the softened peppers and bring to the boil. Stir in the penne, cover and simmer for 5 minutes.

5. Meanwhile, heat a griddle pan until very hot and sear the lamb chops for 1-2 minutes each side.

6. Remove the lid from the pan of peppers and penne and sit the lamb chops on top of the peppers and pasta. Transfer the pan to the oven for about 10 minutes, until the lamb chops are cooked. Serve at once.

COOKING PEPPERS SLOWLY OVER A LOW HEAT, AS HERE, GIVES THEM A DELICIOUS, INTENSE FLAVOUR. WHEN COMBINED WITH THE PENNE THEY MAKE THIS COLOURFUL HOT POT, TOPPED WITH SEARED LAMB.

Pappardelle with salmon & caviare

SERVES 4
175G (6OZ) SMOKED SALMON PIECES
JUICE OF ½ LEMON
FRESHLY GROUND BLACK PEPPER
280G (10OZ) DRIED PAPPARDELLE
40G (1½OZ) UNSALTED BUTTER
4 TEASPOONS BLACK LUMPFISH ROE
1 BUNCH FRESH DILL, CHOPPED
150ML (¼ PINT) SOURED CREAM

1. Preheat the grill to its highest setting.

2. Spread the smoked salmon pieces on the grill pan, squeeze over the lemon juice and season with black pepper. Grill for 4-5 minutes until lightly golden and beginning to crisp.

3. Meanwhile, cook the pasta in a pan of boiling water as directed on the packet.

4. To serve, drain the pasta and toss with the butter, lumpfish roe and dill. Pile the pasta into 4 serving dishes and drizzle over the soured cream. Top each with a mound of grilled salmon and serve at once.

GRILLED, SMOKED SALMON MAY SOUND A LITTLE ODD - HOWEVER IT REALLY IS GOOD, ESPECIALLY WHEN COMBINED WITH PASTA, DILL, SOURED CREAM AND CHEATS' CAVIARE!

Grilled chicken with tahini noodles

SERVES 4

4 CHICKEN BREASTS WITH THE SKIN ON

3 TABLESPOONS HONEY

JUICE OF 1 LIME

FRESHLY GROUND BLACK PEPPER

225G (8OZ) MEDIUM EGG NOODLES

1 TEASPOON SESAME OIL

LIME WEDGES, TO SERVE

FOR THE SAUCE

2 CLOVES GARLIC, CRUSHED

2 TABLESPOONS TAHINI

1½ TABLESPOONS CRUNCHY PEANUT BUTTER

1 TABLESPOON HONEY

2 TABLESPOONS GROUNDNUT OR GRAPESEED OIL

2 TABLESPOONS RICE OR WHITE WINE VINEGAR

1 TABLESPOON DARK SOY SAUCE

100ML (3½FL OZ) WARM WATER

1. Toss the chicken breasts in a dish with the honey and lime juice and season with black pepper. Set aside.

2. Preheat the grill to a medium setting.

3. Place all the sauce ingredients in a food processor and blend until smooth.

4. Grill the chicken breasts for 6-7 minutes each side, or until the juices run clear.

5. When the chicken is nearly ready, cook the noodles in a pan of boiling water as directed on the packet. Very gently heat the sauce in a pan over a low heat, stirring frequently.

6. To serve, drain the noodles and toss with the sesame oil. Arrange on 4 serving plates. Thickly slice each chicken breast and arrange on top of the noodles. Spoon over the warm sauce, place a wedge of lime on each plate and serve at once.

TAHINI CONSISTS SIMPLY OF SESAME SEEDS, GROUND TO A DELICIOUS PASTE. RICH AND TASTY, IT IS USED HERE AS A BASE FOR A NUTTY SAUCE TO ACCOMPANY NOODLES AND GRILLED CARAMELIZED CHICKEN.

Roasted asparagus with pancetta & chive linguini

SERVES 4

2 TABLESPOONS OLIVE OIL

450G (1LB) ASPARAGUS

SALT AND FRESHLY GROUND BLACK PEPPER

350G (12OZ) FRESH LINGUINI

115G (4OZ) PANCETTA LARDONS

JUICE OF 1 LEMON

1 BUNCH FRESH CHIVES, ROUGHLY CHOPPED

FRESH PARMESAN SHAVINGS

LEMON WEDGES, TO SERVE

1. Preheat the oven to Gas Mark 6/200°C/400°F.

2. Pour 1 tablespoon of the oil into a large roasting tray and place in the oven for 2 minutes or until the oil is hot. Lay the asparagus in the tray, season and roast for 10-12 minutes, until just tender and slightly golden.

3. Meanwhile, cook the pasta in a pan of boiling water as directed on the packet.

4. Heat the remaining oil in a large frying pan. Add the lardons and cook for 3-4 minutes, stirring frequently, until crisp and golden. Stir in the lemon juice and remove from the heat. Stir in the chives and season with black pepper.

5. Drain the pasta and return it to the pan in which it was cooked. Toss with the warm pancetta and chive dressing.

6. To serve, divide the pasta between 4 serving plates and arrange the roasted asparagus on top. Top with shavings of Parmesan and serve with lemon wedges.

PANCETTA AND CHIVES MAKE A PERFECT DRESSING FOR LIGHT LINGUINI, WHICH IS DELICIOUS TOPPED WITH ROASTED ASPARAGUS.

Black in red soup

SERVES 2

1 TABLESPOON OLIVE OIL

2 LARGE RED PEPPERS, DESEEDED AND
   COARSELY CHOPPED

1 LARGE ONION, COARSELY CHOPPED

1 CLOVE GARLIC, PEELED

300ML (½ PINT) TOMATO PASSATA

SALT AND FRESHLY GROUND BLACK PEPPER

85G (3OZ) DRIED SQUID INK SPAGHETTI

2 TABLESPOONS SOURED CREAM

2 TABLESPOONS FRESH BASIL LEAVES

1. Preheat the oven to Gas Mark 6/200°C/400°F.

2. Toss together the oil, peppers, onion and garlic in a roasting tin. Roast in the oven for 25-30 minutes, until softened and just beginning to colour.

3. Remove and discard the garlic. Transfer the peppers and onion to a food processor and blend together. Add the passata and season. Blend again and transfer to a small pan.

4. Cook the pasta in a pan of boiling water as directed on the packet, while you gently heat the red 'soup'.

5. To serve, spoon the 'soup' into 2 serving bowls. Drain the pasta and place a pile in the centre of each bowl. Drizzle with the soured cream and garnish with the fresh basil. Serve at once.

THIS DISH LOOKS QUITE DRAMATIC. BE GENEROUS WITH THE BASIL AND SERVE WITH PLENTY OF GARLIC BREAD!

Chicken & cashews on noodles with grilled pineapple

SERVES 4

1 SMALL PINEAPPLE, CORED AND CUT INTO THIN
  WEDGES

2 TEASPOONS RUNNY HONEY

2 TABLESPOONS GRAPESEED OIL

3 LARGE SKINLESS, BONELESS CHICKEN
  BREASTS, CUBED

1 BUNCH SPRING ONIONS, CHOPPED

1 CLOVE GARLIC, CRUSHED

250G (9OZ) MEDIUM EGG NOODLES

JUICE OF 2 ORANGES

6 TABLESPOONS BLACK BEAN SAUCE

100G (3½OZ) CASHEW NUTS, TOASTED

1 BUNCH FRESH CORIANDER LEAVES

1. Preheat the grill to a medium setting.

2. Brush the pineapple wedges with a little runny honey and grill for 3-4 minutes each side, until toasted and golden.

3. Heat the oil in a large wok and add the chicken pieces, spring onions and garlic. Stir-fry for 4-5 minutes, until the chicken is just cooked.

4. Meanwhile, cook the noodles in a pan of boiling water as directed on the packet.

5. Mix together the orange juice and black bean sauce, and stir into the cooked chicken. Simmer for 1 minute then stir in the toasted cashew nuts and coriander leaves.

6. To serve, drain the cooked noodles and divide between 4 serving dishes. Spoon the chicken in black bean sauce on top and serve with the toasted pineapple wedges.

THIS IS A MODERN VERSION OF THE CHINESE CLASSIC.

7 Pasta salads

Like many others, my childhood salads were a sad affair, consisting mainly of limp lettuce and soggy sliced cucumber, dyed pink with beetroot juice. Thank goodness things have changed for the better! Not just for hot summer days, the modern salad has little in common with its humble origins - it is a now gourmet treat that is on the agenda all year round. The selection of tasty dressings and contrasting combinations of flavours and textures in this chapter make salads an appetizing alternative for a wholesome lunch or dinner. Hot, warm or cold, these scrumptious salads offer a variety of pastas and noodles, partnered with roast beef and pesto, artichokes and wild mushrooms and pears and Roquefort and are guaranteed to satisfy the strongest hunger pangs and the most discerning palate.

Crispy pasta salad

SERVES 4

OIL FOR DEEP-FRYING

115G (4OZ) FRESH EGG FUSILLI

SALT

1 SMALL COS LETTUCE, ROUGHLY TORN

55G (2OZ) WATERCRESS

8 RASHERS SMOKED STREAKY BACON, GRILLED
   UNTIL CRISP AND ROUGHLY BROKEN UP

1 AVOCADO, STONED, PEELED AND SLICED

A FEW CURLS OF PARMESAN CHEESE

FOR THE GARLIC DRESSING

150ML (1/4 PINT) SOURED CREAM

1 LARGE BUNCH FRESH CHIVES, CHOPPED

1 CLOVE GARLIC, CRUSHED

SALT AND FRESHLY GROUND BLACK PEPPER

1. Heat the oil in a large deep saucepan or deep fat-fryer. Take 25g (1oz) of the fresh fusilli and fry for about 30 seconds, until crisp and lightly golden. Drain immediately on kitchen paper and sprinkle with a little salt. Repeat with batches of the remaining pasta.

2. Combine all the dressing ingredients in a small bowl and season. Set aside.

3. To serve, arrange the cos lettuce leaves and watercress on a large platter. Scatter over the grilled bacon, the avocado and crispy pasta. Finish with a few curls of Parmesan and serve the garlic dressing separately.

HOT CRISPY PASTA WITH BACON AND AVOCADO AND CURLS OF PARMESAN CHEESE - MOUTHWATERINGLY GOOD! NOTE THAT THE PASTA USED FOR DEEP-FRYING MUST BE FRESH.

Super seedy noodles

SERVES 4

350G (12OZ) WHITE CABBAGE, VERY FINELY
    SHREDDED

1 BUNCH SPRING ONIONS, FINELY SLICED, THE
    GREEN TOPS FINELY SLICED AND RESERVED

1 LARGE CARROT, PEELED AND GRATED

4 TABLESPOONS MAYONNAISE

1 DESSERTSPOON DARK SOY SAUCE

SALT AND FRESHLY GROUND BLACK PEPPER

25G (1OZ) SUNFLOWER SEEDS, TOASTED

25G (1OZ) SESAME SEEDS, TOASTED

15G (½OZ) POPPY SEEDS, TOASTED

250G (9OZ) MEDIUM EGG NOODLES

1. Combine the shredded cabbage, the white spring onion slices, grated carrot, mayonnaise and soy sauce in a large bowl and season. Set aside.

2. Combine all the seeds in another bowl and set aside.

3. Cook the noodles in a pan of boiling water, as directed on the packet. Drain well then toss with the cabbage mixture.

4. To serve, pile the noodle mixture into individual serving bowls. Scatter each with a generous tablespoon of toasted seeds and garnish with the reserved green spring onion tops.

THIS IS A SEEDY NOODLE VERSION OF COLESLAW. TO TOAST THE POPPY, SUNFLOWER AND SESAME SEEDS AND GIVE THEM A FAR BETTER FLAVOUR, DRY-FRY THEM IN A FRYING PAN OVER A MEDIUM HEAT FOR 2-3 MINUTES UNTIL LIGHTLY TOASTED. TRY THIS METHOD FOR OTHER NUTS AND SEEDS.

Roast beef pasta

SERVES 4
225G (8OZ) SIRLOIN STEAK
2 TABLESPOONS WORCESTERSHIRE SAUCE
280G (10OZ) DRIED VERMICELLI
4 HEAPED TABLESPOONS FRESH PESTO
115G (4OZ) SUGAR SNAP PEAS
115G (4OZ) CHERRY TOMATOES, HALVED
SALT AND FRESHLY GROUND BLACK PEPPER
1 BUNCH FRESH BASIL LEAVES

1. Place the steak in a shallow dish. Spoon the Worcestershire sauce over the steak and set aside.

2. Cook the vermicelli in a pan of boiling water, as directed on the packet. When cooked, drain well, toss with the pesto and set aside.

3. Plunge the sugar snap peas into boiling water. Cook for 2-3 minutes, drain and refresh under cold water.

4. Heat a griddle pan until very hot and cook the steak to your liking. The timing will depend on the thickness of your steak - about 1-2 minutes each side for rare steak, 2-3 minutes for medium and 3-4 for well done.

5. To serve, arrange the dressed pasta on a large serving dish. Lightly season the cherry tomatoes and sugar snap peas and scatter over the pasta. Carve the sirloin steak into slices, arrange over the top of the vegetables and serve at once, with the basil leaves scattered over the top.

YOU CAN BUY REALLY GOOD FRESH PESTO FROM SOME SUPERMARKETS AND DELICATESSENS. HOWEVER, MAKING YOUR OWN WITH A FOOD PROCESSOR IS REALLY EASY (SEE PAGE 81).

Niçoise pasta salad

SERVES 4

225G (8OZ) NEW POTATOES, PARBOILED FOR
    5 MINUTES AND HALVED IF LARGE

1 TABLESPOON OLIVE OIL

SALT AND FRESHLY GROUND BLACK PEPPER

225G (8OZ) DRIED TRICOLORE PASTA
    (CONCHIGHLIE, FUSILLI OR FARFALLE)

125G (4OZ) FINE GREEN BEANS

1 x 200G (7OZ) CAN TUNA IN OIL, DRAINED

2 EGGS, HARD-BOILED AND ROUGHLY CHOPPED

FOR THE DRESSING

1 SHALLOT, FINELY CHOPPED

2 TABLESPOONS GREEK-STYLE BLACK OLIVES,
    PITTED AND ROUGHLY CHOPPED

2 TABLESPOONS BABY CAPERS

90ML (3FL OZ) OLIVE OIL

SQUEEZE OF LEMON JUICE

1 BUNCH FRESH FLAT-LEAF PARSLEY, CHOPPED

1. Preheat the oven to Gas Mark 6/200°C/400°F.

2. Toss the potatoes and the oil together in a roasting tin. Season and roast for 30-35 minutes, until lightly golden and cooked.

3. Meanwhile, cook the pasta in a pan of boiling water as directed on the packet.

4. Plunge the beans into boiling water, cook for 3-4 minutes, drain and refresh under cold water.

5. Combine all the dressing ingredients together in a bowl and season. Set aside.

6. To serve, drain the pasta and toss with the dressing and blanched green beans. Transfer to a large serving platter. Scatter over the drained tuna and the chopped egg, and top with the roasted new potatoes. Serve at once.

FRESH TUNA CAN BE USED IN PLACE OF CANNED IF YOU LIKE. SIMPLY FRY OR GRIDDLE SEASONED TUNA STEAKS IN A LITTLE OLIVE OIL FOR 2-3 MINUTES EACH SIDE AND SERVE WITH THIS DELICIOUS POTATO SALAD.

Noodles, crab & cress

SERVES 4

225G (8OZ) MEDIUM EGG NOODLES

2 X 170G (5¾OZ) CANS CRAB MEAT, DRAINED
    AND ROUGHLY FLAKED

2 PUNNETS MUSTARD AND CRESS, SNIPPED

LEMON WEDGES, TO SERVE

FOR THE SAUCE

4 TABLESPOONS MAYONNAISE

2 TABLESPOONS GREEK YOGURT

JUICE OF ½ LEMON

SALT AND FRESHLY GROUND BLACK PEPPER

1. Start by mixing together the sauce ingredients in a bowl and set aside.

2. Cook the noodles in a pan of boiling water as directed on the packet.

3. To serve, drain the noodles and toss with the reserved sauce and the flaked crab meat. Pile into serving bowls and scatter over the mustard and cress. Place a lemon wedge on each and serve at once.

DON'T JUST USE MUSTARD AND CRESS FOR THE OCCASIONAL SANDWICH! IT MAKES AN EXCELLENT PARTNER TO SWEET CRAB AND GIVES A GOOD CLEAN, CRISP FINISH TO THIS TASTY NOODLE SALAD.

Pear & Roquefort rigatoni

SERVES 4

350G (12OZ) DRIED RIGATONI

2 TABLESPOONS POPPY SEEDS

150ML (¼ PINT) FRENCH DRESSING

2 RIPE DESSERT PEARS, CORED AND THICKLY
    SLICED

115G (4OZ) ROQUEFORT CHEESE, CRUMBLED

SALT AND FRESHLY GROUND BLACK PEPPER

1 LARGE BUNCH WATERCRESS, TO SERVE

1. Cook the rigatoni in a pan of boiling water as directed on the packet.

2. Meanwhile, heat a large pan and add the poppy seeds. Gently fry for 1 minute. Add the French dressing to the pan - beware, it may splutter alarmingly - and then add the sliced pears. Simmer for 2 minutes.

3. To serve, drain the cooked pasta and toss well with the pear and poppy seed dressing. Allow to cool slightly for 5 minutes, then gently toss with the crumbled Roquefort. Season to taste and serve at once surrounded by the watercress.

ROQUEFORT HAS TO BE ONE OF MY ALL-TIME FAVOURITE CHEESES. MADE FROM EWE'S MILK, THIS POWERFUL, VEINED CHEESE MARRIES WELL WITH FRUIT, ESPECIALLY PEARS.

Mustard chicken on avocado tagliatelle

SERVES 4

2 LARGE CHICKEN BREASTS, CUT INTO THIN
STRIPS

2 TABLESPOONS GRAINY MUSTARD

1 TABLESPOON HONEY

JUICE OF ½ LEMON

SALT AND FRESHLY GROUND BLACK PEPPER

350G (12OZ) FRESH EGG TAGLIATELLE

4 TABLESPOONS FRENCH DRESSING

1 LARGE AVOCADO, STONED

¼ ICEBERG LETTUCE, SHREDDED

1 TABLESPOON OLIVE OIL

1 TABLESPOON SESAME SEEDS, TOASTED (SEE
PAGE 112)

1. Toss together the chicken, mustard, honey and lemon juice in a bowl. Season and set aside.

2. Cook the pasta in a pan of boiling water as directed on the packet, then drain and toss with the French dressing. Season lightly and set aside.

3. Using a teaspoon remove the avocado flesh in scoops, toss with the shredded lettuce and season.

4. Heat the oil in a large wok. Add the strips of chicken with all of the marinade and stir-fry for 5-6 minutes until the chicken is cooked.

5. To serve, toss the dressed pasta with the avocado and lettuce and divide between 4 plates. Spoon over the hot chicken and scatter with the toasted sesame seeds. Serve at once.

THIS IS A SCRUMPTIOUS DISH OF SIZZLING STRIPS OF MUSTARD CHICKEN TOSSED WITH AVOCADO AND TAGLIATELLE!

Chargrilled chicken with apricot & cumin pasta

SERVES 4

3 SKINLESS, BONELESS CHICKEN BREASTS

2 TABLESPOONS OLIVE OIL

JUICE OF ½ LEMON

FRESHLY GROUND BLACK PEPPER

350G (12OZ) DRIED FARFALLE

SALT

55G (2OZ) PINE NUTS, TOASTED (SEE PAGE 112)

FOR THE DRESSING

150ML (¼ PINT) OLIVE OIL

JUICE OF 1 LEMON

JUICE OF 1 ORANGE

1 TABLESPOON GROUND CUMIN, TOASTED

115G (4OZ) READY-TO-EAT DRIED APRICOTS, CHOPPED

1 BUNCH FRESH MINT, CHOPPED

1. Lay each chicken breasts between 2 layers of non-pvc clear film or greaseproof paper and, using a rolling pin, beat until about 5mm (¼ inch) thick. Place the chicken in a dish and pour over the olive oil and lemon juice. Season with black pepper and set aside for 1 hour.

2. Cook the pasta in a pan of boiling water as directed on the packet. Mix all the dressing ingredients together in a large bowl. When the pasta is cooked, drain and toss with the dressing. Season well and set aside.

3. To serve, heat a griddle pan until very hot. Sear the chicken breasts for 2-3 minutes each side until cooked, then cut up into rough strips. Pile the dressed pasta on to one large serving dish or 4 smaller ones. Scatter over the griddled chicken and finish with the toasted pine nuts, sprinkled on top.

TRY THIS PASTA, ALL DRESSED UP WITH A SPICY, FRUIT DRESSING, TOPPED WITH GRIDDLED STRIPS OF CHICKEN AND A SPRINKLING OF TOASTED PINE NUTS. TO TOAST THE CUMIN SEEDS, GENTLY DRY-FRY THEM IN A SMALL PAN OVER MEDIUM HEAT FOR 30 SECONDS.

Artichoke & mushroom salad with mimosa

SERVES 4

450G (1LB) DRIED TRICOLORE PASTA

1 x 285G (10¼OZ) JAR ANTIPASTO
   ARTICHOKES, DRAINED

1 x 290G (10¾OZ) JAR ANTIPASTO MIXED WILD
   MUSHROOMS, DRAINED

1 TABLESPOON BALSAMIC VINEGAR

SALT AND FRESHLY GROUND BLACK PEPPER

2 EGGS, HARD-BOILED AND FINELY CHOPPED

1 BUNCH FRESH FLAT-LEAF PARSLEY, CHOPPED

1. Cook the pasta in a pan of boiling water as directed on the packet. When cooked, drain and toss with the artichokes, mushrooms and balsamic vinegar. Season well and set aside for at least 2 hours or in the refrigerator overnight.

2. To serve, toss the chopped egg and parsley together in a bowl. Pile the pasta salad on to a large serving dish and scatter over the egg and parsley mimosa topping.

THESE JARS OF ANTIPASTO VEGETABLES, WHICH ARE NOW WIDELY AVAILABLE, ARE SUPERB FOR ADDING INSTANT FLAVOUR AND ZEST TO PASTA DISHES.

Roasted Madras salmon salad

SERVES 4

3 TEASPOONS MADRAS CURRY PASTE

JUICE OF ½ LEMON

4 x 115G (4OZ) SALMON FILLETS

225G (8OZ) DRIED PAPPARDELLE

115G (4OZ) CUCUMBER, FINELY CHOPPED

1 BUNCH SPRING ONIONS, CHOPPED

175ML (6FL OZ) GREEK YOGURT

SALT AND FRESHLY GROUND BLACK PEPPER

1. Preheat the oven to Gas mark 6/200°C/400°F.

2. Mix 1 teaspoon of the curry paste with the lemon juice in a small bowl. Place the salmon fillets on a lightly greased baking tray and brush with the curry and lemon paste. Bake for about 15 minutes, until the salmon is opaque and just cooked.

3. Meanwhile, cook the pasta in a pan of boiling water as directed on the packet.

4. Mix the remaining curry paste in a bowl with the cucumber, spring onions and Greek yogurt and season well.

5. To serve, drain the cooked pasta and toss with the madras yogurt dressing. Pile on to 4 serving plates and top each with a fillet of salmon. Serve at once.

THIS IS A QUICK AND SIMPLE WAY OF COOKING SALMON. OVERCOOKED SALMON CAN BE DRY, SO REMEMBER TO SLIGHTLY UNDERCOOK YOUR FISH, AS IT WILL CONTINUE TO COOK ONCE REMOVED FROM THE OVEN.

8

Pasta for One

Home alone with your favourite pasta? Time to yourself at last! Uncork the wine and have a relaxing bath. Then head for the kitchen, prepare some pasta, then select your ingredients and dress it up! For me, this minimal style of cooking and dressing pasta is one of the very best. Each of the dressing recipes in this chapter combines with 115g (4oz) of your favourite pasta to serve one. If you have company, simply double up the quantities - but be prepared to share! By choosing some of the most delicious ingredients, you can treat yourself to dishes fit for the most stylish of dinner parties. And with no one to please but yourself, you have free choice as to which particular pasta will best compliment the ingredients and suit your own mood and taste.

Garlic & herb butter

SERVES 1

115G (4OZ) DRIED OR FRESH PASTA

25G (1OZ) BUTTER

1 SMALL CLOVE GARLIC, CRUSHED

1 TABLESPOON CHOPPED FRESH FLAT-LEAF
  PARSLEY

1 HEAPED TABLESPOON CHOPPED FRESH CHIVES

15G (½OZ) FRESHLY GRATED PARMESAN
  CHEESE

SALT AND FRESHLY GROUND BLACK PEPPER

1. Cook the pasta in a pan of boiling water as
   directed on the packet. Drain and toss with the
   butter, garlic, parsley, chives and Parmesan.
   Season to taste and serve at once.

TRY SMOKED GARLIC IN PLACE OF THE USUAL GARLIC FOR
A VARIATION ON THIS BUTTER. IT IS ALSO GREAT SPREAD
ON LARGE HUNKS OF TOAST OR SERVED MELTING OVER
LARGE GRILLED FLAT MUSHROOMS.

Anchovy & caper

SERVES 1

115G (4OZ) DRIED OR FRESH PASTA

15G (½OZ) BUTTER

1 x 50G (1¾OZ) CAN ANCHOVY FILLETS IN
  OLIVE OIL, DRAINED AND CHOPPED

1 TABLESPOON CAPERS, RINSED

15G (½OZ) FRESHLY GRATED PARMESAN
  CHEESE

FRESHLY GROUND BLACK PEPPER

1 TABLESPOON CHOPPED FRESH FLAT-LEAF
  PARSLEY

1. Cook the pasta in a pan of boiling water as directed on the packet.

2. Meanwhile, heat the butter in a small pan. Add the chopped anchovies and gently fry for 2-3 minutes. Remove from the heat and add the capers.

3. To serve, drain the pasta and toss with the anchovy and caper butter and grated Parmesan. Season with black pepper and scatter over the flat-leaf parsley. Serve at once.

INSTEAD OF TOSSING WITH FRESHLY COOKED PASTA, THIS TASTY BUTTER CAN BE SERVED ON A BAKED POTATO TOPPED WITH TUNA FISH AND SALAD.

Grainy mustard & tarragon

SERVES 1

115G (4OZ) DRIED OR FRESH PASTA

2 TEASPOONS GRAINY MUSTARD

2 TABLESPOONS CRÈME FRAÎCHE

½ TEASPOON CHOPPED FRESH TARRAGON LEAVES

SALT AND FRESHLY GROUND BLACK PEPPER

1. Cook the pasta in a pan of boiling water as directed on the packet.

2. Meanwhile, mix together the mustard, crème fraîche and chopped tarragon in a bowl. Season well.

3. To serve, drain the pasta and toss with the mustard and tarragon dressing. Grind over a little black pepper and serve at once.

IDEAL WITH PASTA, THIS IS ALSO EXCELLENT SERVED AS A SIDE SAUCE WITH ROAST CHICKEN OR GRILLED FISH.

Cheddar & walnut

SERVES 1

115G (4OZ) DRIED OR FRESH PASTA

½ TABLESPOON WALNUT OIL

½ TABLESPOON GRAPESEED OIL

40G (1½OZ) CHEDDAR CHEESE, GRATED

SALT AND FRESHLY GROUND BLACK PEPPER

2 TABLESPOONS CHOPPED FRESH FLAT-LEAF
   PARSLEY

1. Cook the pasta in a pan of boiling water as directed on the packet. Drain and toss with the oils and grated Cheddar. Season well, scatter with the chopped parsley and serve.

THIS RECIPE ALSO MAKES A RICH DRESSING FOR A SALAD OF CRISP COS LEAVES, HOT CROUTONS, SLICED APPLES AND BACON BITS.

Chilli, lime & coriander

SERVES 1

115G (4OZ) DRIED OR FRESH PASTA

25G (1OZ) BUTTER

1 RED CHILLI, DESEEDED AND FINELY CHOPPED

2 TABLESPOONS CHOPPED FRESH CORIANDER

SQUEEZE OF LIME JUICE

SALT AND FRESHLY GROUND BLACK PEPPER

1. Cook the pasta in a pan of boiling water as directed on the packet. Drain the pasta and toss with the butter, chilli, coriander and lime juice. Season and serve at once.

AN ALTERNATIVE USE FOR THIS BUTTER MIXTURE IS TO SPREAD IT OVER A PORTION OF SALMON FILLET, AND ROAST IN THE OVEN UNTIL THE FISH IS JUST COOKED.

Black olive & feta

SERVES 1

115G (4OZ) DRIED OR FRESH PASTA

1 TABLESPOON SUN-DRIED TOMATO OIL

6 GREEK-STYLE BLACK OLIVES, PITTED AND CHOPPED

1 SMALL CLOVE GARLIC, CRUSHED

1 TABLESPOON CHOPPED FRESH PARSLEY

15G (½OZ) FETA CHEESE, CRUMBLED

FRESHLY GROUND BLACK PEPPER

1. Cook the pasta in a pan of boiling water as directed on the packet. Drain and toss with the oil, chopped olives, garlic and parsley. Scatter over the feta cheese, season with black pepper and serve at once.

USE THE OIL FROM A JAR OF SUN-DRIED TOMATOES FOR THIS RECIPE. THIS DRESSING IS DELICIOUS TOSSED WITH PASTA, STIRRED INTO MASHED POTATOES OR SPOONED OVER A BAKED POTATO.

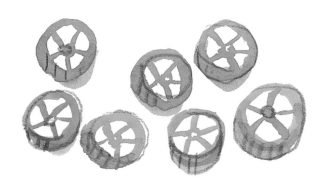

Harissa butter

SERVES 1

115G (4OZ) DRIED OR FRESH PASTA

1 HEAPED TEASPOON HARISSA PASTE

85G (3OZ) CANNED CHICK PEAS, DRAINED AND
   RINSED

15G (½OZ) UNSALTED BUTTER

2 TABLESPOONS WHITE WINE

2 TABLESPOONS OF FLAT LEAF PARSLEY,
   CHOPPED

1. Cook the pasta in a pan of boiling water as directed on the packet.

2. While the pasta is cooking, heat a small pan. Add the harissa paste and gently fry-dry for 30 seconds.

3. Add the chick peas to the pan and toss well together. Add the butter and stir until the butter has melted. Simmer for 3-4 minutes.

4. To serve, drain the pasta and toss with the harissa chick peas and the parsley. Serve at once.

Vinegar tomatoes with pecorino

SERVES 1

115G (4OZ) DRIED OR FRESH PASTA

1 TABLESPOON OLIVE OIL

115G (4OZ) BABY PLUM OR CHERRY TOMATOES,
   HALVED

GOOD PINCH OF SUGAR

SALT AND FRESHLY GROUND BLACK PEPPER

1 TABLESPOON BALSAMIC VINEGAR

SHAVINGS OF PECORINO CHEESE TO SERVE

1. Cook the pasta in a pan of boiling water as directed on the packet.

2. While the pasta is cooking, heat the oil in a small frying pan. Add the tomatoes and sugar and season. Fry over the high heat for 30-60 seconds, until the tomatoes are heated through but still hold their shape. Remove from the heat and immediately stir in the balsamic vinegar.

3. To serve, drain the pasta and transfer to a serving dish. Spoon over the vinegar tomatoes and scatter over the pecorino shavings. Serve at once.

125

Roasted hazelnut & spring onion

SERVES 1

115G (4OZ) DRIED OR FRESH PASTA

55G (2OZ) HAZELNUTS, ROASTED

25G (1OZ) RED LEICESTER CHEESE, GRATED

2 SPRING ONIONS, FINELY CHOPPED

1 TABLESPOON OLIVE OIL

SALT AND FRESHLY GROUND BLACK PEPPER

1. Cook the pasta in a pan of boiling water as directed on the packet. Drain and toss with the hazelnuts, grated red Leicester, spring onions and olive oil. Season and serve at once.

THE RED LEICESTER CHEESE WITH ITS SWEET BUTTERY LEMON TASTE AND THE ROASTED HAZELNUTS REALLY BRING THIS PASTA TO LIFE. SERVE WITH PASTA; IT IS ALSO EXCELLENT WITH GRIDDLED FISH.

Stilton & watercress

SERVES 1

115G (4OZ) DRIED OR FRESH PASTA

½ BUNCH WATERCRESS, THICK STALKS REMOVED

1½ TABLESPOONS OLIVE OIL

1 TEASPOON LEMON JUICE

SALT AND FRESHLY GROUND BLACK PEPPER

25G (1OZ) STILTON, CRUMBLED

1. Cook the pasta in a pan of boiling water as directed on the packet.

2. Place the watercress, olive oil and lemon juice in a small food processor. Blend until the watercress is finely chopped and then season well.

3. To serve, drain the pasta and toss with the dressing. Sprinkle the Stilton over the top and serve at once.

9

The unexpected

This chapter is dedicated to breaking the mould. Pasties, frittatas and even pasta desserts - the sky's the limit! As these recipes prove once again, pasta is a delicious staple and a great carrier of flavours. Sweet or spicy, you'll be amazed how wonderfully versatile it can be! Serve a pasta dessert for a change - a lemon lasagne or pasta baked with peaches may sound odd, even shocking to some people, but they're definitely worth trying for yourself!

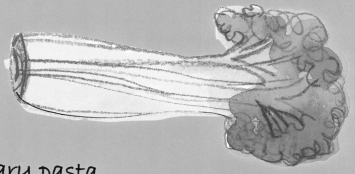

Bloody Mary pasta

SERVES 4

1 RED PEPPER, HALVED

½ TABLESPOON OLIVE OIL

125ML (4FL OZ) TOMATO PASSATA

1 x 400G (14OZ) CAN CHOPPED TOMATOES IN
   TOMATO JUICE

DASH OF TABASCO SAUCE

DASH OF WORCESTERSHIRE SAUCE

CELERY SALT AND FRESHLY GROUND BLACK
   PEPPER

GENEROUS SLUG OF VODKA

350G (12OZ) TORTELLINI

1. Preheat the oven to Gas Mark 6/200°C/400°F.

2. Place the red pepper on a baking tray and drizzle with the olive oil. Roast in the oven for 25-30 minutes, until the skin is charred.

3. Peel the roasted pepper and roughly chop the flesh. Place in a food processor with the passata, canned tomatoes, Tabasco sauce and Worcestershire sauce. Season with celery salt and black pepper and blend together until smooth. Stir in the vodka.

4. Transfer the sauce to a saucepan and simmer for 5 minutes. Meanwhile, cook the tortellini in a pan of boiling water as directed on the packet.

5. To serve, drain the tortellini and place in a large serving dish. Take to the table with the hot pan of bloody Mary and allow everyone to dip their pasta into it.

IF YOU HAVE A PASSION FOR VODKA, YOU'LL LOVE THIS! AS AN ALTERNATIVE YOU COULD MAKE UP THIS SAUCE AND SERVE IT AS A COLD DIP ACCOMPANIED BY PIPING HOT TORTELLINI FOR A REAL KICK!

Pasta pasties

MAKES 8

115G (4OZ) DRIED MACARONI OR ANY SMALL
PASTA

1 TABLESPOON OLIVE OIL

250G (9OZ) BABY SPINACH, ROUGHLY
SHREDDED

250G (9OZ) RICOTTA CHEESE

6 SUN-DRIED TOMATOES IN OIL, DRAINED AND
ROUGHLY CHOPPED

4 SLICES PARMA HAM, SHREDDED

2 TABLESPOONS ROUGHLY CHOPPED FRESH BASIL

SALT AND FRESHLY GROUND BLACK PEPPER

450G (1LB) READY-MADE PUFF PASTRY

1 EGG, BEATEN

CRISP GREEN SALAD , TO SERVE

CHUTNEY, TO SERVE

1. Preheat the oven to Gas Mark 7/220°C/425°F.

2. Cook the pasta in a pan of boiling water as directed on the packet and drain well.

3. Meanwhile, heat the oil in a large frying pan. Add the spinach and toss over a high heat until wilted. Transfer to a bowl and allow to cool, before adding the ricotta, sun-dried tomatoes, Parma ham, chopped basil and cooked pasta. Mix together and season well.

4. Roll out the puff pastry on a lightly floured surface until about 3mm ($\frac{1}{8}$ inch) thick. Cut into 8 approximately 13cm (5 inch) squares. Divide the pasta mixture equally among the squares, spooning it on to the centre of each square. Brush the pastry edges with a little beaten egg and bring the corners of each square to the centre, pressing the edges together to form a parcel.

5. Transfer the parcels to a baking tray and brush with more beaten egg. Bake in the oven for 12-15 minutes, until puffed and golden, and serve warm or cold with a crisp green salad and chutney.

THIS IS A CONTINENTAL VERSION OF A CORNISH PASTY AND A GREAT WAY OF USING UP LEFTOVER PASTA.

Blt frittata

SERVES 4

85G (3OZ) DRIED MACARONI

250G (9OZ) CHERRY TOMATOES

1 TABLESPOON BALSAMIC VINEGAR

2 TABLESPOONS OLIVE OIL

SALT AND FRESHLY GROUND BLACK PEPPER

1 BUNCH FRESH BASIL LEAVES

4 EGGS

150ML (¼ PINT) DOUBLE CREAM

3 SLICES PARMA HAM, SHREDDED

25G (1OZ) BUTTER

55G (2OZ) GRUYÈRE CHEESE, GRATED

55G (2OZ) ROCKET LEAVES

1. Cook the macaroni in a pan of boiling water as directed on the packet. Drain well and set aside.

2. Meanwhile, preheat the oven to Gas Mark 6/200°C/400°F. Preheat the grill to a medium setting.

3. Place the cherry tomatoes in a roasting tin and spoon over the balsamic vinegar and half of the olive oil. Season and place in the oven to roast for 15-20 minutes.

4. While the tomatoes are roasting, place the basil, eggs and double cream in a food processor. Blend together then stir in the shredded Parma ham and cooked macaroni, and season.

5. Heat the remaining oil with the butter in a large non-stick frying pan. Pour in the macaroni and egg mixture and cook over a medium heat until the base is golden - check this by lifting the edge carefully with a palette knife. Scatter the Gruyère over the top and place the pan under the grill until golden and bubbling hot.

6. To serve, slide the omelette on to a large serving platter, top with the rocket leaves and spoon over the roasted cherry tomatoes with any pan juices. Serve at once.

THIS RICH PASTA OMELETTE IS FLAVOURED WITH BASIL, CHEESE AND PARMA HAM. TOPPED WITH ROCKET AND BAKED TOMATOES, IT IS UTTERLY DELICIOUS!

Souffléed Stilton vermicelli with celery & apple relish

SERVES 6

175G (6OZ) DRIED VERMICELLI

SALT

55G (2OZ) BUTTER

2 TABLESPOONS DRIED BREADCRUMBS

55G (2OZ) PLAIN FLOUR

600ML (1 PINT) MILK

175G (6OZ) STILTON, CRUMBLED

6 EGGS, SEPARATED

FRESHLY GROUND BLACK PEPPER

FOR THE RELISH

4 CELERY STICKS, ROUGHLY CHOPPED

2 DESSERT APPLES, CORED AND ROUGHLY
  CHOPPED

1 SMALL RED ONION, ROUGHLY CHOPPED

JUICE OF 1 LEMON

1 BUNCH FRESH FLAT-LEAF PARSLEY, ROUGHLY
  CHOPPED

1. Preheat the oven to Gas Mark 6/200°C/400°F.

2. Crush and break the pasta into a pan of boiling salted water and cook as directed on the packet. Drain well.

3. Melt the butter in a saucepan. Using a pastry brush, brush a large shallow ovenproof dish with a little of the melted butter and dust lightly with the dried breadcrumbs. Set the dish aside.

4. Stir the flour into the remaining melted butter in the pan and cook gently for 45 seconds. Remove from the heat and gradually whisk in the milk. Return to the heat and, stirring continuously, simmer for 2 minutes until the sauce is very thick and smooth. Remove from the heat and stir in the cheese, the egg yolks and the cooked pasta. Season well.

5. In a large bowl, whisk the egg whites until stiff, but not dry. Mix 1 tablespoon of the egg whites into the cheese and pasta mixture, then fold in the remaining egg white and transfer the mixture to the prepared soufflé dish. Place in the oven and bake for 20-25 minutes, until golden and puffed.

6. Meanwhile, place all the relish ingredients except the parsley in a food processor and process until well combined. Stir in the roughly chopped parsley and season to taste.

7. To serve, remove the soufflé from the oven and serve at once with the relish.

YES, THIS IS A SOUFFLÉ WITH A DIFFERENCE - USING PASTA THE STILTON GIVES IT A RICH FLAVOUR AND THE CELERY RELISH PROVIDES A REALLY FRESH CLEAN KICK.

Thai-style pasta paella

SERVES 4

1 TABLESPOON VEGETABLE OIL

1 BUNCH SPRING ONIONS, CUT INTO STRIPS
    LENGTHWAYS

2-3 TEASPOONS RED THAI CURRY PASTE

2 KAFFIR LIME LEAVES, CRUMBLED

250G (9OZ) DRIED CONCHIGLIETTE (TINY PASTA
    SHELLS)

600ML (1 PINT) VEGETABLE STOCK

150ML (¼ PINT) COCONUT MILK

350G (12OZ) SALMON FILLET, SKINNED AND
    CUT INTO 2.5CM (1 INCH) CUBES

115G (4OZ) RAW TIGER PRAWNS, PEELED WITH
    TAILS LEFT ON

200G (7OZ) FINE GREEN BEANS

1 BUNCH FRESH CORIANDER, ROUGHLY CHOPPED

SALT AND FRESHLY GROUND BLACK PEPPER

4 LIME WEDGES, TO SERVE

1. Heat the vegetable oil in a large pan or wok. Add the spring onions and fry for 2 minutes. Add the Thai curry paste, lime leaves and pasta and stir together well.

2. Pour in three-quarters of the stock and the coconut milk and bring to the boil. Cover and simmer for 5 minutes.

3. Meanwhile, plunge the beans into boiling water, cook for 3-4 minutes, drain and refresh under cold water.

4. Remove the lid from the pan or wok and stir in the cubes of salmon and the prawns. Cook, uncovered, for a further 3-4 minutes, until the fish and pasta are cooked, adding more stock if the mixture becomes too dry. Two minutes before the end of the cooking time, stir in the blanched green beans.

5. To serve, stir the fresh coriander through the 'paella', season to taste and spoon into individual serving dishes. Add a wedge of lime to each dish and serve at once.

Ricotta & conchellini-filled omelette

SERVES 2

55G (2OZ) DRIED CONCHELLINI (TINY PASTA SHELLS)

55G (2OZ) RICOTTA CHEESE

55G (2OZ) GRUYÈRE CHEESE, FINELY GRATED

55G (2OZ) SHREDDED SPINACH

SALT AND FRESHLY GROUND BLACK PEPPER

SQUEEZE OF LEMON JUICE

4 EGGS, BEATEN

1 TABLESPOON WATER

GRATING OF FRESH NUTMEG

15G (½OZ) BUTTER

1. Cook the pasta in a pan of boiling water as directed on the packet.

2. Meanwhile, combine the ricotta and Gruyère cheeses, spinach and lemon juice in a bowl. Season well and set aside. Combine the eggs, water and nutmeg in another bowl and season well.

3. Heat half the butter in a large omelette pan until foaming. Pour in half the egg mixture and cook until the bottom is golden and the top just set. Meanwhile, drain the pasta and quickly combine with the spinach and cheese mixture.

4. Transfer the omelette to a warmed serving plate. Pile half the pasta filling on to one half of the omelette and flip the other half of the omelette over to cover the filling.

5. Heat the remaining butter in the pan and cook a second omelette in the same way. Fill as before and serve them at once.

THIS UNUSUAL OMELETTE IS DELICIOUS SERVED WITH A SALAD OF VERY THINLY SLICED BEEFSTEAK TOMATOES, SPRINKLED WITH A LITTLE BALSAMIC VINEGAR, ROCK SALT, BLACK PEPPER AND A TOUCH OF OLIVE OIL.

Vermicelli suzette

SERVES 4

1 x 411g (14½oz) CAN MANDARIN ORANGES
  IN NATURAL JUICE, DRAINED WITH THE JUICE
  RESERVED

ABOUT 425ML (¾ PINT) ORANGE JUICE

25g (1oz) UNSALTED BUTTER

55g (2oz) CASTER SUGAR

GRATED RIND OF 1 ORANGE

2 x 55g (2oz) DRIED VERMICELLI PASTA
  'NESTS'

1 TABLESPOON BRANDY

2 TABLESPOONS GRAND MARNIER

VANILLA ICE CREAM OR SINGLE CREAM, TO
  SERVE

1. Combine the reserved mandarin orange juice in a jug with enough orange juice to make up to 600ml (1 pint).

2. Melt the butter with the caster sugar and orange rind in a large shallow pan. Add the mandarin and orange juice and simmer for 5 minutes.

3. Meanwhile, using a sharp, serrated knife, cut each vermicelli nest in half horizontally to form 4 small nests. Place in a shallow dish and cover with boiling water. Set aside for 3 minutes.

4. Drain the pasta nests and sit them in the pan containing the orange juice. Combine the brandy and Grand Marnier and tip into a metal ladle or a small pan. Hold over the hob to heat gently then carefully ignite the alcohol. Pour the flaming alcohol over the nests. Spoon a little of the hot pan liquid over the nests, cover with a lid and cook for 3-5 minutes, or until the pasta is cooked.

5. To serve, spoon the nests and orange sauce on to serving plates, scatter over the mandarin segments and serve at once with vanilla ice cream or single cream.

THE RICH, BUTTERY ORANGE SAUCE OF THIS FRENCH CLASSIC MAKES A PERFECT DESSERT WHEN COMBINED WITH VERMICELLI PASTA NESTS. FLAME WITH BRANDY AND SERVE WITH TOP-QUALITY VANILLA ICE CREAM.

Cinnamon & honey pasta with vanilla ice cream

SERVES 4

1 TEASPOON CINNAMON

4 TEASPOONS CASTER SUGAR

OIL FOR DEEP-FRYING

350G (12OZ) FRESH RICCIOLI

4 TABLESPOONS RUNNY HONEY

VANILLA ICE CREAM, TO SERVE

1. Toss together the cinnamon and sugar in a bowl.

2. Heat the oil for deep-frying in a large saucepan or a deep fat-fryer. Deep-fry the pasta in batches of no more than 85g (3oz) at a time for about 2 minutes, until crisp. Drain on kitchen paper.

3. Place the hot crispy pasta on 4 serving plates. Drizzle over the runny honey and sprinkle with the cinnamon and sugar mixture. Serve at once with vanilla ice cream.

THIS DELICIOUS DESSERT OF HOT CRISPY PASTA ROLLED IN HONEY AND SPICE, SERVED WITH ICE CREAM, IS TO DIE FOR!

Amaretti peach gratin

SERVES 6-8

175G (6OZ) DRIED BABY MACARONI

400ML (14FL OZ) FRESH CUSTARD

115G (4OZ) AMARETTI BISCUITS, ROUGHLY
 CRUSHED

4 RIPE PEACHES OR NECTARINES, HALVED AND
 STONED

25G (1OZ) DEMERARA SUGAR

3 TABLESPOONS AMARETTO LIQUER (OPTIONAL)

1. Preheat the oven to its highest setting.

2. Cook the macaroni in a pan of boiling water as directed on the packet and drain well.

3. Combine the cooked pasta with the custard and Amaretti biscuits and transfer to a shallow ovenproof dish. Top with the peach or nectarine halves, cut-side up and sprinkle with the sugar.

4. Place the dish on the highest oven shelf and bake for 10-15 minutes, until the contents are bubbling hot and the fruit is caramelized.

5. Remove from the oven. Transfer the Amaretto, if using, to a ladle. Hold over the hob and gently heat, then carefully ignite before pouring over the fruit. Serve at once.

AMARETTI BISCUITS WITH PEACHES IS A MATCH MADE IN HEAVEN - ESPECIALLY WHEN FLAMBÉED WITH AMARETTO.

Pasta au citron

SERVES 4

4 LARGE SHEETS FRESH EGG LASAGNE

6 TABLESPOONS GOOD-QUALITY LEMON CURD

300ML (½ PINT) DOUBLE CREAM

GRATED RIND OF 1 ORANGE

¼ TEASPOON FRESHLY GRATED NUTMEG

2 FRESH RIPE MANGOES, PEELED, STONED AND
   CUT INTO CHUNKS

2 LARGE ORANGES, PEELED AND SEGMENTED

15G (½OZ) DEMERARA SUGAR

1. Preheat the oven to Gas Mark 6/200°C/400°F.

2. Soak the lasagne sheets as directed on the packet
   and drain well.

3. Gently combine the lemon curd with the cream in
   a large bowl. Add the orange rind and grated
   nutmeg.

4. Take one-third of the mango chunks and the
   orange segments and place in the base of a
   shallow ovenproof dish. Spoon over one-third of the
   lemon custard and lay over 2 sheets of lasagne.
   Repeat these 3 layers, then top the lasagne with a
   final layer of custard and then the remaining
   fruit. Scatter the demerara sugar over the top.

5. Place in the oven and bake for 20-25 minutes
   until golden and bubbling hot. Serve at once.

GOOD-QUALITY LEMON CURD IS A MUST FOR THIS SWEET
DISH, WHICH IS BAKED WITH SLICES OF RIPE RICH MANGO.

Pasta rice pudding

SERVES 4

115G (4OZ) SULTANAS

115G (4OZ) READY-TO-EAT DRIED APRICOTS,
CHOPPED

GRATED RIND AND JUICE OF 1 ORANGE

225G (8OZ) QUICK-COOK BABY MACARONI

¼ TEASPOON FRESHLY GRATED NUTMEG

450G (1LB) GOOD-QUALITY VANILLA ICE CREAM,
ROUGHLY MASHED WITH A FORK

1 TABLESPOON DEMERARA SUGAR

1. Mix together the sultanas, apricots, orange rind and juice in a large bowl. Set aside for 30 minutes.

2. Preheat the oven to Gas Mark 5/190°C/375°F.

3. Cook the macaroni in a pan of boiling water as directed on the packet and drain well. Toss the cooked macaroni with the fruits, orange rind and juice, the nutmeg and the ice cream. Transfer to an ovenproof dish.

4. Bake for 10 minutes, then remove from the oven and stir. Sprinkle over the demerara sugar and return to the oven for 20 minutes. Serve at once.

FORGET THE RICE AND PLUNGE IN PASTA INSTEAD TO MAKE A GREAT BRITISH PUDDING WITH A CONTINENTAL TWIST.

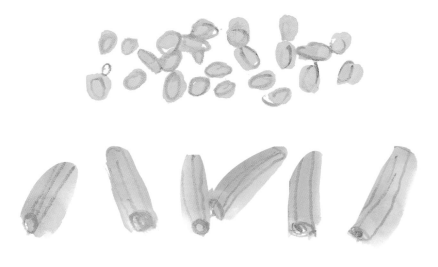

Open blueberry & apple frittata

SERVES 6

55G (2OZ) DRIED MACARONI

115G (4OZ) MASCARPONE CHEESE

4 EGGS, BEATEN

200G (7OZ) BLUEBERRIES

25G (1OZ) CASTER SUGAR

1 TEASPOON CINNAMON

2 TABLESPOONS RUNNY HONEY

3 COX APPLES, CORED AND THICKLY SLICED

25G (1OZ) BUTTER

ICING SUGAR TO DUST

1. Cook the macaroni in a pan of boiling water as directed on the packet. Drain and leave to cool.

2. Meanwhile, beat the mascarpone in a large bowl and slowly mix in the beaten eggs.

3. Using the back of a spoon, gently bruise half of the blueberries and stir into the egg mixture. Then add the caster sugar, cinnamon and cooked macaroni and set aside.

4. Preheat the grill to a medium setting.

5. Melt the honey in a frying pan. Add the apple slices and fry over a high heat for 6-8 minutes until slightly coloured and tender. By resisting the temptation to stir frequently you will allow the apples to slightly caramelize. Stir in the remaining whole blueberries and cook for 1 minute.

6. Meanwhile, heat the butter in a large non-stick frying pan and pour in the mascarpone and pasta mixture. Cook over a medium heat for about 5 minutes, until golden underneath - check this by carefully lifting the edge with a palette knife. Transfer the pan to the grill and cook until golden on top.

7. To serve, remove the pan from the grill and spoon the hot honeyed apples and blueberries over the frittata. Dust with icing sugar, take to the table and serve at once straight from the pan.

CARAMELIZED APPLES AND BLUEBERRIES TOP A HOT MASCARPONE, BLUEBERRY AND PASTA FRITTATA!

10

cook's Tips

A little knowledge can be a valuable thing - and this is certainly true in the kitchen. Of the many tips up my sleeve, passed on by friends, family and colleagues over the years, I have listed here just a few quick and easy favourites. These little gems of advice should save you time, effort and make cooking for all occasions an altogether more pleasurable experience. I hope you find them as useful as I have done. Happy cooking!

- USE A DRY PASTRY BRUSH FOR QUICK AND EASY REMOVAL OF ORANGE OR LEMON RIND FROM A GRATER.

- BEFORE USING SPICES, DRY-FRY THEM IN A PAN OVER A GENTLE HEAT FOR A FEW SECONDS TO BRING OUT THE FLAVOUR. BE CAREFUL NOT TO BURN THEM.

- TO PREVENT SALT GOING DAMP, A FEW GRAINS OF RICE ADDED TO YOUR SALT SHAKER WILL ABSORB ANY MOISTURE AND ALLOW THE SALT TO RUN FREELY.

- ALWAYS STORE OLIVE OIL IN A COOL DARK PLACE, AWAY FROM DIRECT HEAT OR SUNLIGHT, AND KEEP IT WELL SEALED.

- TO STOP YOUR CHOPPING BOARD SMELLING OF GARLIC AFTER CRUSHING CLOVES, PLACE A SQUARE OF GREASEPROOF PAPER ON YOUR BOARD, BENEATH THE CLOVE AND CRUSH IT ON TO THE PAPER.

- SHELLFISH SHOULD ALWAYS BE USED ON THE DAY OF PURCHASE.

- REMOVE ALL PLASTIC WRAPPING FROM PURCHASED FRUIT AS SOON AS YOU GET IT HOME AND STORE IT IN A CLEAN FRUIT BOWL IN A COOL DARK PLACE. NEVER STORE BANANAS IN THE FRIDGE.

- WHOLE SPICES CAN BE GROUND MOST EASILY USING A COFFEE GRINDER.

- RIPEN TOMATOES BY LEAVING THEM ON A SUNNY WINDOWSILL.

- USE AVOCADO WHEN IT IS JUST SOFT ENOUGH TO GIVE SLIGHTLY UNDER PRESSURE FROM YOUR THUMB. OVERSOFT AND BRUISED AVOCADOS HAVE A RANCID BITTER FLAVOUR AND SHOULD NOT BE USED.

- TURN A SHOP-BOUGHT SOUP INTO A MORE NOURISHING MEAL BY ADDING COOKED PASTA OR NOODLES TO IT.

- FOR GOOD FLAVOUR DO NOT OVERCHOP YOUR HERBS - SIMPLY TEAR OR ROUGHLY CHOP THEM.

- TO BRING OUT THE BEST FLAVOUR OF NUTS, SPREAD THEM OUT ON A BAKING SHEET AND ROAST IN A HOT OVEN UNTIL LIGHTLY COLOURED BUT DO NOT ALLOW THEM TO BURN OR BECOME BITTER.

Index